LOOKING AT TYPE SERIES

Looking at Type in the Workplace

by Larry Demarest

CENTER FOR APPLICATIONS OF PSYCHOLOGICAL TYPE, INC.
GAINESVILLE, FLORIDA

Published by
Center for Applications of Psychological Type, Inc.
2815 NW 13th Street, Suite 401
Gainesville, FL 32609
(352) 375-0160

Printed in the United States of America.

ISBN 0-935652-32-9

Contents

Introduction

The differences among people are one of the most fascinating—and most perplexing—aspects of daily life. Our understanding of and reaction to others is a key to both our effectiveness and satisfaction on the job. Working productively and smoothly together requires that we understand ourselves as well as our co-workers.

The Myers-Briggs Type Indicator® is a self-report instrument that is widely used to help people gain insight into their own psychological preferences and the preferences of others. The MBTI® helps people identify their habitual practices in four arenas of life. Its four scales are briefly described on the next page.

The MBTI scales are bipolar and the theory underlying the instrument assumes that in each of the paired dichotomies, people prefer one mode over the other. Our psychological type is expressed as the combination our preferred modes indicate on each of the scales. (For in-depth explanations of the fundamentals of psychological type, Charles Martin's *Looking at Type: The Fundamentals* and Gordon Lawrence's *People Type and Tiger Stripes* are helpful resources.)

Looking at Type in the Workplace is an introduction to how individuals' psychological types affect their daily interactions at work. Its three sections provide:

1) Descriptions of how the characteristics of the 16 types are typically expressed at work,

2) Information about the patterns of psychological types of five groups found in many organizations—managers, secretaries, marketing personnel, accountants, and computer professionals—and,

3) Discussion of how our psychological type can influence everyday workplace activities such as responding to conflict, work style, being part of a team, making decisions, dealing with change, and communication.

The MBTI Preference Scales

The direction of your energy and attention

People with a preference for extraversion focus their attention on the outer world and are energized by interaction and activity.

People with a preference for introversion focus their attention on their inner world and are energized by reflection and solitude.

The way you like to take in information (the kind of perception you prefer to use)

People with a preference for sensing become aware *directly* through the five senses. They naturally turn first to, are most interested in, and put the most trust in concrete and verifiable information about what is or what has been.

People with a preference for intuition become aware indirectly through hunches, imagination, "ahas", and inspiration. They naturally turn first to, are most interested in, and put the most trust in flashes of insight, abstractions, theory, and notions of what could be.

How you like to make decisions or come to closure (the kind of judgment you prefer to use)

People with a preference for thinking decide based on logic and analysis of causes and effects. For them, a good decision is one that "makes sense".

People with a preference for feeling decide based on human values and the anticipated effects of the decision on people. For them, a good decision is one that "feels right".

How you like to live your life in the outer world

People with a preference for judging like to reach closure, to decide, and to approach life in an orderly and structured fashion.

People with a preference for perceiving like to gather information and generate alternatives, to keep their options open as long as possible, and to approach life in an unstructured and flexible manner.

Type at Work

How can knowing about psychological type help us understand people at work? To help make type come alive in the workplace, work-focused descriptions of each of the eight MBTI preference scales and each of the 16 types are included.

In the following section, The Eight Preferences at Work (as well as in several other places), the four preference scales are described separately, i.e., extraversion is contrasted with introversion, sensing with intuition, thinking with feeling, and judging with perceiving. This is done for explanatory purposes, in order to focus on the dichotomies between each pair of characteristics and to begin to see how the elements of type may appear at work.

In a sense though, it is artificial to isolate the preference scales in this way because the dimensions of type do not occur separately. They are always an integral part of a whole type. Take, for example, a person who has preferences for introversion, sensing, thinking, and judging, referred to as ISTJ. The ISTJ type does not result from simply adding I + S + T + J. Rather, ISTJ is a unique and dynamic combination of those four dimensions into a distinctive system. Although ISTJ might appear to be just one letter different from INTJ, the changing of that one "letter" from S to N creates a different dynamic whole called INTJ.

There is a section called May Be Experienced As in each of the preference descriptions and type descriptions. It is tricky to describe how others may experience a person with differing preferences (or even someone with the same preferences). For one thing it simply is difficult to describe the world from another's vantage.

In addition, what might be relatively "objective" behavior (i.e., behavior we could all agree happened if we observed it on a video tape) is filtered through one's own preferences (and other "filters") and may be quickly interpreted or judged. For example, one person may double check to be sure that the figures in a report are correct. Some team members may experience this as "being a stickler for details" or "nitpicking" while others are appreciative that someone is attending to having the figures correct.

Projection is another factor in how we experience others. When we experience a particular characteristic (or lack of it) in others, we may actually be projecting something about ourselves on to the other person. A Sally Forth cartoon I enjoy provides a good example. At the beginning of a three-day weekend, Sally asks her husband Ted what he has on his agenda. Ted responds that he doesn't have an agenda for the weekend, to which Sally replies, "How can you function without an agenda?" While this appears to be a statement about Ted, it is really a statement about Sally's preference to have a plan for her weekend, i.e., it is a projection.

Despite these hurdles in describing how we may experience others and how they may experience us, it seems appropriate to include this material as a basis for self-awareness and for discussion and feedback among colleagues.

Following the section on the Eight Preferences at Work you will find full length descriptions of the sixteen types in the section The Sixteen Types at Work. Each description is shown next to its opposite type and near to its "cousin type." The positioning invites the contrast and comparison that are so useful in finding the best-fit type.

The Eight Preferences At Work

EXTRAVERSION
at work

People with a preference for extraversion focus their attention on the outer world and are energized by interaction and activity.

A person who prefers extraversion...

What You Might Notice First
- is someone who reaches understanding through interaction and discussion, is someone who wants to talk it through
- willingly engages and involves others
- is energetic and prone to take action

Work Style
- creates opportunities to be involved with others from the outset of a project or assignment
- moves around and may "do business" in various locations
- welcomes people "stopping by" or calling to touch base or chat
- prefers physical space which facilitates interaction

In Groups/On Teams
- participates, often speaks up right away
- lets others know what s/he thinks or feels
- seeks, gives, and desires more feedback
- regards meetings as places to build relationships and as vehicles to get work done

During Change
- has radar to scan the external world and responds to guidance from the environment—-co-workers, customers, the market, trends
- sees others as an important resource, seeks input from others, and talks with them about change as it is occurring
- wants to move ahead, to make a decision or try something

During Conflict
- expresses self—thoughts, feelings, possible solutions
- engages with others to consider the conflict
- prefers to discuss and deal with conflict now

Contributions
- is energetic and enthusiastic
- is aware of the impact of what's going on in the larger organization and the outside world
- makes headway which comes from the inclination to take action and get things done

May Be Experienced As
- energetic, sociable, making things happen, involving others and *sometimes* as overwhelming others with their energy and enthusiasm, asking a lot of questions (some of which might seem personal), moving rapidly from one topic or activity to another, persistently advocating their own ideas or positions

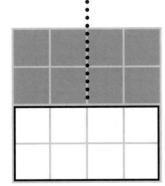

The Eight Preferences At Work

Introversion
at work

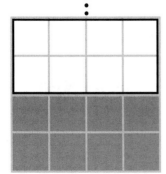

People with a preference for introversion focus their attention on their inner worlds and are energized by reflection and solitude.

A person who prefers introversion...

What You Might Notice First

- is someone who reaches understanding by contemplating and mulling things over, is someone who wants to think about it
- seems less engaged, even when around others
- is reflective and prone to consider before acting

Work Style

- works alone at first, involving others after one's own ideas or position have been formulated
- stays in own area and others may need to go there to conduct business
- experiences people who "stop by" or call to chat as interruptions
- prefers physical space which allows for privacy and concentration

In Groups/On Teams

- participates and speaks up after observing and formulating own impressions and questions
- may need to be asked what s/he thinks or feels
- seeks, gives, and desires less feedback
- regards meetings as taking time away from work and as places where more work gets generated or assigned

During Change

- has an internal gyroscope to keep self on track and responds to the guidance of one's own vision, standards, experience, sensations
- sees own self as the primary resource and keeps own counsel or seeks advice from a few confidants; often communicates only after reflecting, perhaps not until after the change has occurred
- wants to be deliberate about making a decision or trying something

During Conflict

- seeks time to sort out thoughts and feelings and to formulate solutions
- withdraws from others to consider the conflict
- wants to discuss it later (sometimes not at all)

Contributions

- is calm, cool-headed
- is aware of internal guiding principles, philosophy, and commitments
- provides perspective which comes from the inclination to "take-a-step-back" and reason things through

May Be Experienced As

- quiet, stable, thoughtful, deep and sometimes as disinterested, tending to keep to themselves, less active than others, not naturally sharing much information

The Eight Preferences At Work

SENSING at work

People with a preference for sensing become aware directly through the five senses. They naturally turn first to, are most interested in, and put the most trust in concrete and verifiable information about what is or what has been.

A person who prefers sensing...

What You Might Notice First

- focuses first on and is most interested in specifics and the details of current or past reality; notices the "trees" before noticing the "forest"
- communicates straightforwardly
- is realistic, practical, and works with "what is"

Work Style

- works at a steady pace
- prefers—and gives—complete instructions indicating both the end result and the specifics about how to get there
- works on one thing at a time
- likes to begin from and use what is already known

In Groups/On Teams

- wants the team to have a clear purpose and goals
- needs accurate information in order to move ahead confidently
- wants the work of the team to be realistic and doable, and is less interested in (and may be impatient with) discussions about vague, unrealistic, or "theoretical" possibilities
- takes things literally, at face value

During Change

- seeks to retain elements that have been shown to be valuable, tried and true ("If it ain't broke, don't fix it.")
- favors change which builds on existing footings and past experiences, and speaks in terms such as "incremental change" or "continuous improvement"
- wants to know how the change will actually be carried out and to see an example of it

During Conflict

- experiences conflict as rooted in the specifics of particular events
- seeks a complete and accurate account of what has happened
- offers practical solutions which may seem to others to miss the underlying point

Contributions

- is aware of the current situation and provides data for group deliberations
- brings previous experience to bear on work at hand
- keeps things grounded

May Be Experienced As

- down-to-earth, meticulous, reminding others of what is practical and realistic, able to enjoy the present moment and *sometimes* as not giving much attention to the long range view, paying too much attention to details, overlooking on the underlying meanings or patterns, wanting to continue to do what has been shown to work rather than try something with no track record

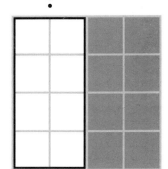

The Eight Preferences At Work

i**N**tuition
at work

People with a preference for intuition become aware indirectly through hunches, imagination, "ahas", and inspiration. They naturally turn first to, are most interested in, and put the most trust in flashes of insight, abstractions, theory, and notions of what could be.

A person who prefers intuition...

What You Might Notice First
- focuses first on and is most interested in the big picture, global issues, future possibilities; notices the "forest" before noticing the "trees"
- communicates in general terms with fewer details
- is speculative and works toward "what if"

Work Style
- works in bursts, awaits inspiration, may skip around, pursuing what "strikes my fancy"
- prefers—-and gives—-general instructions, indicating the end result but not necessarily how to get there
- may work on several things at the same time
- elects to acquire new knowledge that is interesting even if there is no apparent use for it

In Groups/On Teams
- wants the team to have an engaging vision and mission
- is comfortable moving ahead with little or incomplete information
- initiates and enjoys consideration of possibilities or theoretical matters—-assumes there's a way to get it done once we're clear about the concept
- takes things figuratively and looks for a "deeper" meaning

During Change
- welcomes, creates, is enthusiastic about change, and is excited by future possibilities ("If it ain't broke, break it.")
- envisions broad, sweeping, fundamental changes, and speaks in terms such as "paradigm shift" and "transformative change"
- assumes there's a way to bring change about—-"We'll work out the details later."

During Conflict
- experiences conflict as growing out of differing interpretations of patterns of events
- seeks to comprehend and delve into the significance of what has happened
- posits general solutions which may seem vague to others

Contributions
- provides a vision of the future, a long range view
- arouses energy and zeal, especially for pursuing the mission and for innovations
- creates a synthesis of data, ideas, and viewpoints

May Be Experienced As
- full of ideas and options, rising to a challenge (especially an intellectual one), looking to the future, seeing connections among seemingly unrelated things and *sometimes* as overlooking the facts or generalizing from only a few facts, communicating indirectly (skipping around and changing topics), making proposals that seem impossible to carry out, exaggerating

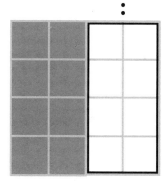

The Eight Preferences At Work

THINKING at work

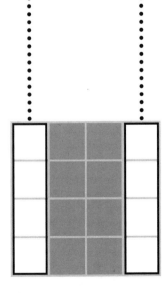

People with a preference for thinking decide based on logic and analysis of causes and effects. For them, a good decision is one that "makes sense".

A person who prefers thinking...

What You Might Notice First
- may seem distant and/or unapproachable
- typically responds by first asking questions and challenging what is said
- is direct, sometimes at the cost of being insensitive to others

Work Style
- focuses on the work at hand; doesn't allocate much time to get to know others and build relationships
- has interactions that are often brief and to the point
- is naturally critical of ideas and proposals, and often makes suggestions for "how to improve" things
- wants expectations, organizational structure, decisions, procedures, etc. to "make sense"

In Groups/On Teams
- believes that <u>what</u> is accomplished is more important than <u>how</u> the group works together, and so pays less attention to and places less importance on the "people" parts of work
- expects the best ideas and solutions to emerge from argument and debate, and enjoys give and take
- wants feedback to focus on results and to identify weaknesses and areas for improvement; may distrust or discount too much positive feedback
- believes that having business-like working relationships is a prerequisite to being able to focus effectively on the task

During Change
- bases actions on principles and tries to remain objective, even about personal change
- isn't particularly concerned with how others have dealt with similar situations
- believes that organizational change should be undertaken for "business" reasons and to meet system needs

During Conflict
- accepts that conflict is a normal part of work and doesn't necessarily expect or need it to be resolved, hence, may not consider it urgent to deal with conflict
- may not be aware that others are experiencing discord and may be less comfortable with "people" aspects of conflict
- works toward solutions that are fair and based on principles that can be applied in similar situations

Contributions
- analyzes objectively—-is able to step back and be impartial
- identifies deficiencies in ideas and plans, and impediments to achieving goals
- champions sticking to the principles

May Be Experienced As
- an independent thinker, task-oriented, skeptical, analytical and *sometimes* as making suggestions for improvement that are experienced as criticism by others, direct to the point of being blunt, sarcastic, distant and "cool"

The Eight Preferences At Work

FEELING
at work

People with a preference for feeling decide based on humane values and the anticipated effects of the decision on people. For them, a good decision is one that "feels right".

A person who prefers feeling...

What You Might Notice First

- is amiable and approachable
- typically responds by first looking for common ground and expressing agreement or sharing concern
- is sensitive to others, sometimes at the cost of being direct

Work Style

- often wants to spend some time getting to know others and build relationships before getting to the work at hand
- has interactions that encompass both work and non-work matters
- is naturally appreciative of people's ideas and contributions
- wants expectations, organizational structure, decisions, procedures, etc. to "feel right" to themselves and others

In Groups/On Teams

- believes that how the group works together and the interpersonal climate are equally important as what is accomplished; pays more attention to and places greater value on the "people" parts of work
- expects the best ideas and solutions to emerge from cooperation and building on everyone's contributions; may experience give and take arguments as disruptive
- prefers receiving regular feedback that acknowledges contributions and fosters growth and development
- believes that having harmonious working relationships is a prerequisite to being able to focus effectively on the task

During Change

- bases actions on subjective values and how people have been affected and will be affected
- wants to know how others have dealt with similar situations
- is comfortable basing change on the experiences or needs of individuals

During Conflict

- experiences conflict as disruptive to working relationships, and wants to resolve it so that the team can get on with its work
- serves as a barometer for group climate, and often is the first to be aware that there is conflict; may be negatively affected even though the conflict doesn't directly involve them
- places more importance on resolutions that feel right to those involved and respond to the particular situation; seeks win/win results

Contributions

- is sensitive to how others will react or be affected
- promotes harmony, conciliation, and well-being
- urges actions that are congruent with individual values and the professed values of the organization

May Be Experienced As

- people-oriented, affirming, supportive of others, sympathetic and *sometimes* as not making the "tough" decisions (not "sticking to their guns"), giving more attention to people and relationships so they may not seem to "get down to business", taking things personally when they weren't intended to be, "illogical"

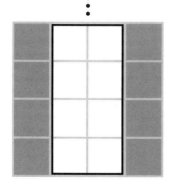

The Eight Preferences At Work

JUDGING
at work

People with a preference for judging like to reach closure, to decide, and to approach life in an orderly and structured fashion.
A person who prefers judging...

What You Might Notice First
- has or wants a plan and may be uncomfortable proceeding without one
- uses terms suggesting a definite result, e.g., "goal", "objective", "outcome"
- is decisive and deliberate
- is serious

Work Style
- is methodical and systematic, and often develops routine approaches to work
- likes to finish things—may do so even when finishing is no longer appropriate or necessary
- brings a structure (e.g., categories, a model, a checklist) to the work at hand
- sees work and play as distinct aspects of life, assuming that (for the most part) play should take place outside of work or at designated events (such as holiday parties or office picnics)

In Groups/On Teams
- takes a "let's get on with it/let's get it done" stance, and may frustrate others by deciding "too quickly" without "sufficient" input and discussion of alternatives
- works best when there is something definite to work toward (e.g., a goal, deadline, milestone); wants the group to focus on and organize to accomplish the agreed-upon result
- wants to be sure everyone knows the expectations and standards and that each member carries out their responsibilities and keeps commitments
- initially responds to a new task or assignment with, "There's no way we can take on a new project," then later adjusts plans and schedules to fit it in

During Change
- often experiences change as disruptive, even change that is seen as necessary
- assumes there is a best approach to take or a "right way" to go about the change
- wants to plan the change in order to minimize false starts and unanticipated events

During Conflict
- begins consideration of the conflict from one point of view or perspective
- has a preferred solution or proposed course of action in mind; seems firm about own view, apparently leaving little room for flexibility or negotiation
- may find it a challenge to set own position aside to consider other options

Contributions
- is decisive and has a drive to "get on with it"
- supports planning
- perseveres—sticks to commitments, plans, and schedules

May Be Experienced As
- dependable, deliberate, conclusive, focused and *sometimes* as taking things "too seriously", deciding too quickly, demanding, and being so focused on goals they have set that they miss out on other things

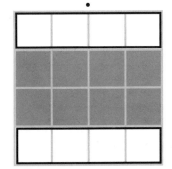

The Eight Preferences At Work

PERCEIVING
at work

People with a preference for perceiving like to gather information and generate alternatives, to keep their options open as long as possible, and to approach life in an unstructured and flexible manner.

A person who prefers perceiving...

What You Might Notice First

- waits to see what unfolds, and is comfortable proceeding without a definite plan
- uses terms suggesting a general course, e.g., "direction", "thrust", "approach"
- is open, receptive, and exploratory
- seems less serious, more playful and lighthearted

Work Style

- is adaptable and often devises flexible or innovative approaches to work
- likes to start things—motivation and interest may decline when it's time to finish
- uses approaches or processes which emanate from experiences with the work at hand
- sees work and play as intertwined aspects of life, and wants work to be productive, enjoyable and playful

In Groups/On Teams

- takes a "let's wait and see what rolls out" approach; may frustrate others by bringing up new information or possibilities after a decision seems to have been made
- is comfortable not having something definite to work toward, and may feel constrained by what they perceive to be narrow or rigid goals and deadlines; wants the group to focus on processes and to organize around ways they will work together (e.g., gathering information, making decisions)
- initially welcomes a new assignment or project, thinking there's lots of time to get it done—and later may feel pushed to fit everything in

During Change

- welcomes the excitement and opportunities that accompany change
- trusts that the best way to carry out the change will emerge from the experiences and needs of those involved
- finds unanticipated events interesting and a source of learning

During Conflict

- seeks out various perspectives from which to understand people or events
- proposes alternative approaches that flexibly incorporate multiple viewpoints
- may need to make an effort to be clear about which alternative they themselves prefer

Contributions

- brings in new information, perspectives, and options
- incorporates the unanticipated and promotes taking changing circumstances into account
- has fun and encourages others to do so too

May Be Experienced As

- spontaneous, "go with the flow", open to new experiences and not wanting to miss out on anything, fun loving, and *sometimes* as having difficulty deciding, tentative, less organized than others, being "last minute"

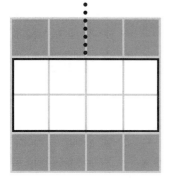

The Sixteen Types At Work

EN**T**Js at work

Thinking
Intuition
Sensing
Feeling

What You Might Notice First
- are tough-minded, logical, and critical
- are energetic and action-oriented, take the initiative and get things organized, quick and decisive
- are articulate and assertive, have definite opinions, are often clever with words and sometimes brusque
- are confident, responsible, hard working, and get a lot done

Work Style
- want their work to be challenging and to provide opportunities to develop and advance, like their accomplishments to be visibly acknowledged
- are self-starters who build—but don't necessarily maintain—structures and systems
- place great value on competence, prefer to work with masterful and ambitious people, may become impatient or intolerant of irresponsibility or incompetence
- set and meet objectives, generally follow procedures unless they interfere with accomplishing goals, and are frustrated by lack of action or closure

In Groups/On Teams
- are goal-oriented, want to stick to the job and get it done, are anxious when things are not getting done, and will not let the group flounder
- are always looking for a better way so they critique and then generate ideas and propose plans to address problems or make improvements
- are gregarious but not necessarily warm, and may be uncomfortable with small talk
- often have or assume authority; question authority when they don't have it

During Change
- perform well in a crisis
- able to deal with complexity and handle multiple factors at the same time
- believe that change can be managed rationally by utilizing plans, structures, and models
- prone to introduce change when leading; but may be less comfortable when not in control or when there is ambiguity

During Conflict
- see "conflict" as a problem to be solved, a situation to get beyond, or something to negotiate; are not uncomfortable "agreeing to disagree" or living with tensions such as a "personality differences"
- may overlook process issues and the other "people parts" of conflicts, and may have difficulty understanding, accepting, and dealing with feeling values
- may be viewed by others as the cause of conflict due to their drive to critique and improve systems and people
- under stress, may focus even more strongly on the task; may have an uncharacteristic flare-up of feelings—explode or attack—-or cover up their own feelings with humor

Contributions
- broad vision and the ability to anticipate and plan for long-term organizational challenges
- initiative to move the team or organization in new directions, to attempt the seemingly impossible
- willingness and the ability to make and stand by tough decisions
- understanding of power and how to use it, political astuteness, and ability to work within the structure

May Be Experienced As
- great at running things and *sometimes* as imposing ideas on others or making decisions for them
- decisive and *sometimes* as concluding too quickly, after considering too few options
- very focused on the goal or task and *sometimes* as so intent on reaching their aim that they are not sensitive to others' concerns, are impersonal, critical, or impatient
- career and work-oriented and *sometimes* as being too serious, not playing enough

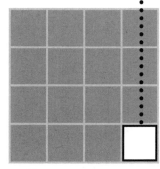

The Sixteen Types At Work

IS**F**Ps at work

Feeling

Sensing

Intuition

Thinking

What You Might Notice First

- are kind, warmhearted, caring, accepting, tolerant, and patient
- are reserved, unassuming, unceremonious, and may appear laid back
- in their work areas, they may have distinctive features which reflect people, animals, or concerns important to them
- are realistic and observant, particularly attentive to what's going on with people

Work Style

- want to be helpful, want their work to foster and further their people-oriented values in tangible ways
- have an active, hands-on style, and place most confidence in what has been learned from direct experience
- are independent, preferring to have freedom from restrictive structures and rules, but also like to be involved with others (though they not necessarily drawn to meetings)
- pay attention to details and can readily work with a lot of specific information

In Groups/On Teams

- prefer a cooperative, supportive, and participatory climate where everyone is regarded as equal and treated with respect
- are excellent gatherers of information, bringing data to bear on team deliberations
- accomplish much that may may go unnoticed since they do little to draw attention to themselves and often work "behind the scenes"
- don't like to give or receive feedback which they regard as criticism; as supervisors, may dislike evaluating others

During Change

- are usually open to change that is congruent with their values and commitments to people, but may have difficulty supporting changes that seem to go against these commitments
- are responsive, flexible, and pragmatic unless a deeply held (and possibly heretofore unexpressed) value is compromised
- focus their attention and energy on actualities and the concerns of the present, and may be less drawn to or comfortable with considering what "might be"
- are reflective, open, and willing to listen to all points of view

During Conflict

- often are barometers for conflict and are aware when discord exists in a relationship or group
- clearly prefer harmony, seek to reach win/win solutions, and may avoid distasteful situations or agree to premature solutions in order to relieve discomfort
- may assume responsibility for fixing what they did not break
- under stress, may be critical toward themselves and/or find fault with others

Contributions

- bring an awareness of people's needs into the day-to-day deliberations of the work place, and naturally appreciate human diversity
- value and demonstrate loyalty to people, groups, and organizations
- champion the spontaneous enjoyment of life, particularly today's special moments
- help keep things running smoothly by unobtrusively carrying out much of the less visible work of organizations

May Be Experienced As

- particularly attentive to the needs of others, often showing they care by doing something special for them and *sometimes* as not assertive enough about their own needs and deeds and having difficulty saying "no"
- so responsive to current needs that they become "side-tracked"
- "free spirits" who take a very personal approach to life and create their own pathway through life's adventure
- having deeply held values which they express through action but don't communicate about very much

The Sixteen Types At Work

ES**T**Js at work

Thinking

Sensing

Intuition

Feeling

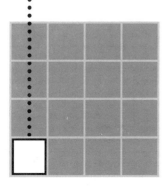

What You Might Notice First

- are goal-directed and task-oriented, take work seriously, and are hard working
- are energetic and action-oriented, have a "get it done" attitude, and love to accomplish things
- are decisive, realistic, and matter-of-fact
- are responsible, reliable, conscientious, and consistently follow through

Work Style

- rely on facts, logic, and experience to make decisions, and have definite criteria for what is correct
- are systematic, structured and efficient; follow rules, procedures, and standard ways; judge work objectively
- like the practical "real world" aspects of work where concrete and useful results are realized, and likes to have clear results to work toward
- prepare thoroughly

In Groups/On Teams

- like a structured environment with clear procedures that can be counted on and clear roles and responsibilities that people are accountable for
- usually have a definite opinion of where the team should head and how it should get there, and focus on goals and objectives to get the group going and keep it on track
- are clear, direct, and often forceful communicators who may offer teammates "constructive criticism" (which is meant to help others fulfill their responsibilities)
- are friendly, but not personal, and prefer to keep discussions centered on the business at hand

During Change

- like stability and order, and are uncomfortable with frequent change or ambiguous situations, and so may respond to change by seeking to impose a structure or plan on it
- respect tradition and "lessons learned", seek to retain what has been shown to work
- have lucid, often strongly held views of what ought to happen
- support change when current practice is illogical, there is a convincing rationale or a tangible improvement can be shown to result; not inclined to support change in the absence of a visible problem or "for the sake of change"

During Conflict

- experience conflict when things are not logical or don't go according to plan, may not regard interpersonal or group process issues as conflict, and are less comfortable when emotions are brought into play
- have a solution in mind and strongly advocate it, and may become frustrated with those with a different view
- may over-depend on past experience when seeking solutions
- under stress, may feel overwhelmed, may become overly sensitive and not feel valued, and may feel uncharacteristically emotional

Contributions

- get things organized, and keep groups and institutions on an even keel
- push for clarity about all things—-goals, roles, assignments, standards, timelines
- being productive and task-oriented—get the job done on time, meeting standards, and within budget
- make efficient and sensible use of resources

May Be Experienced As

- decisive and organized and *sometimes* as closing off options abruptly and leaving others out of the process
- efficient and productive and *sometimes* as impersonal, not warm, and overlooking or devaluing the subjective factors and the interpersonal aspects of working together
- impatient, especially with those regarded as inefficient, lacking direction or common sense, not abiding by the rules, or being too emotional
- having definite viewpoints and *sometimes* as not listening well to ideas which deviate from their own, not responsive to other points of view

The Sixteen Types At Work

IN**F**Ps at work

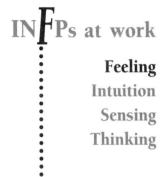

Feeling

Intuition

Sensing

Thinking

What You Might Notice First

- are adaptable, tolerant, receptive, and calm
- are oriented toward the future ("what could be"), and suggest possibilities and options
- often have good communication skills, though they may not communicate much, especially about themselves
- are sensitive to others, congenial, and empathetic

Work Style

- like quiet and alone time for concentration, and may have periods of high activity and productivity followed by apparent lulls
- are most captured by work that has personal meaning or is an expression of "who I am", and helps make the world a better place
- like flexibility, and dislike a lot of routine, structure, and rules (e.g., prescribed procedures and tight timelines)
- are comfortable and patient with complexity, and may overlook details

In Groups/On Teams

- emphasize interpersonal values—-warmth, cooperation, sharing of information, and building trust—-and are aware of and sensitive to "process issues"
- are reflective and insightful—-see patterns and possibilities, and may have a unique or unusual perspective
- like to feel connected to others on the team, seek to create a sense of pulling together, and want others to feel like they belong
- work doggedly, often unobtrusively, for what is important to them

During Change

- are open to change, and naturally look beyond the present to see and create possibilities
- are able to deal with ambiguity, fluidity, and matters "in process"
- favor change that advances "people values" and what feels right for people, and want the process of change to be inclusive and "people friendly"
- protective of their own relationships during change

During Conflict

- don't like interpersonal conflict, and may be thrown off by it or seek to withdraw
- often serve as peacemaker or harmonizer, look for and can usually find an open door in a dilemma or an impasse
- may assume too much personal responsibility for conflict in relationships
- under stress, can become preoccupied, over-react, be difficult to be around, and/or find fault with others

Contributions

- endeavor to create a positive, harmonious environment that fosters the growth and development of people
- interpersonal sensitivity
- adaptability and flexibility (though they are not flexible when integrity is at stake)
- idealism, inspiration, and a deep commitment to values that leads them to expect the organization to live out its own values

May Be Experienced As

- loyal and committed to people and *sometimes* as so committed that they become overextended trying to fulfill promises or please others
- having high expectations, hard on themselves, "perfectionistic"
- postponing making decisions until the "last minute"
- non-conforming when in pursuit of their own inner values or vision

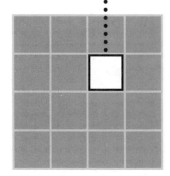

The Sixteen Types At Work

ES*F*Js at work

Feeling
Sensing
Intuition
Thinking

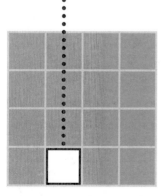

What You Might Notice First

- readily connect with people—are warm-hearted, friendly, outgoing, sensitive, and helpful
- take assignments and responsibilities seriously, are dutiful, conscientious, and dependable
- are active, energetic, and productive
- are decisive and inclined to take action

Work Style

- like direct, cooperative involvement with others, and values above all work that provides tangible benefits to people
- work best within and follow existing structures that help things run smoothly (e.g., procedures, schedules, the chain of command), will create structure when it is missing, and want to know clearly what is expected and how it will be assessed
- follow through—stick with projects to completion
- like to be actively appreciated and recognized for contributions and achievements

In Groups/On Teams

- are good team players who are supportive of others, exert a positive influence, work to have everyone pulling in the same direction, and may be the glue that holds the team together
- favor personable, harmonious, and cooperative environments where people feel part of the group and at ease and where appreciation is expressed for everyone's contributions
- want the team to take action and are themselves impatient with drawn-out philosophical or theoretical deliberations
- are attentive to detail, especially people-oriented detail, and foresee people's needs

During Change

- favor changes that benefit the entire group and change processes where people pull together
- like clear beginnings and endings, and do best when there is time to adjust to new approaches—appear to be less comfortable with ambiguity and the loose ends of transition
- have strong, often traditional values, and may seek to preserve these during change
- if they sense a loss of control, may use authoritative or absolute statements or actions

During Conflict

- place great value on interpersonal harmony and will work hard to find a way for all to be in accord, will try to do or say something to ease the tension, and may agree to a solution that will remove discord for the time being
- may find the conflict that others regard as every day give and take (e.g., people advocating and defending their positions, pointed humor) as troublesome
- seek opportunities to process conflict appropriately, and may be affected negatively or pull back if processing doesn't occur
- under stress, may criticize or blame, may disengage, or may discount the counsel of those they usually respect

Contributions

- help keep things moving efficiently and harmoniously toward agreed upon ends
- provide structure, organize people, and organize for people
- work to balance the needs of people and the organization
- provide stability by drawing on effective past practices and maintaining traditions

May Be Experienced As

- supportive and nurturing of others and *sometimes* as socializing too much or so focused on others' needs that their own needs are not attended to
- preferring and providing structure and *sometimes* as inflexible, not necessarily open to new approaches
- serious and responsible and *sometimes* as "too" responsible, "worriers"
- deciding and acting quickly and *sometimes* as moving ahead hastily, before considering enough data or options

The Sixteen Types At Work

IN**T**Ps at work

Thinking
Intuition
Sensing
Feeling

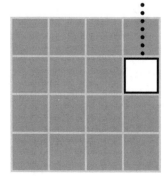

What You Might Notice First
- are concerned with ideas, astute and curious, intellectually inventive, seem to be deep thinkers
- have an opinion about what should be done (e.g., to solve a problem), often challenge others or give advice
- are objective, analytical, and critical about nearly everything
- are less involved and communicative, perhaps aloof or terse

Work Style
- can work alone and concentrate for prolonged periods of time, need private time, and often get absorbed in an idea or project and ignore other things
- want to understand the theory and principles underlying what they do, and to continue learning new things
- are independent and self-directed (prefer to set own goals and standards, and figure out how to meet them) and have a strong need for autonomy (resist rules and hierarchy, and may not be particularly good followers)
- may be satisfied formulating a mental solution and be less interested in implementing it, don't like routine, and may not want to do something a second time once they have learned it

In Groups/On Teams
- generate creative ideas and solutions, are originators and builders of systems, and provide a framework or model to aid understanding of problems
- give more attention to the problem-solving process (e.g., questions posed, data brought to bear) than to achieving a particular result or end point
- want to base team decisions on tough-minded analysis, and will call the group back to the logic of the situation
- often work best alone (though they like to be in interaction with people on the "cutting edge"), not naturally collaborative, may seem to be working alone even when a member of a team, don't give much feedback

During Change
- willing to take risks (though not interpersonal ones), propose unique or unorthodox approaches
- are flexible and adaptable—up to the point where strongly held principles come into play
- look for a logical basis for change, may be impatient with or baffled by non-logical factors (such as politics, emotions, tradition)
- need time to think about change, especially when it involves personal change

During Conflict
- are tolerant and possess a capacity for detachment that allows them to see multiple perspectives and viewpoints
- look for patterns as the key to unlocking conflict, and can re-define problems to make them solvable
- may want to step back to consider their response and develop a strategy
- are not usually comfortable with and don't give much weight to emotions; however, under stress may become emotional themselves, become hyper-logical, or withdraw

Contributions
- understand the big picture and connections among the parts, and see the long range consequences of today's actions
- offer new perspectives and create unique solutions
- are comfortable in handling ambiguity and complexity, and are able to synthesize divergent outlooks
- incisive thinking and critiques—-finds flaws, inconsistencies, contradictions, and gaps in thinking

May Be Experienced As
- insightful and creative (though not necessarily concerned with the usefulness of ideas) and *sometimes* as overly intellectual ("head in the clouds"), having difficulty making ideas and concepts a reality
- not paying enough attention to interpersonal relationships, seeming detached and insensitive
- intense, serious, complicated, and puzzling and *sometimes* as making things too complex, being contentious ("splitting hairs"),
- impatient with or frustrated by those not on their wave length or those who are not as quick as they perceive themselves to be; having unrealistic expectations of self and others

The Sixteen Types At Work

EN**F**Js at work

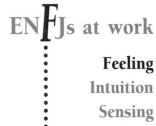

Feeling

Intuition

Sensing

Thinking

What You Might Notice First

- are enthusiastic and energetic, involved with the people and events around them, often in the center of things and sought out by others
- take interest in others and are easy to relate to—-outgoing, naturally engaging, gracious, comfortable and skilled at working with others
- are expressive—-communicate freely and openly, convincing, and self-revealing
- are reliable, responsible, and persistent

Work Style

- work interactively, seek to involve others and be facilitative, create and make use of networks to get work done
- do their best work in a supportive, lively environment where there is a sense of connectedness and a variety of challenges
- like things to be organized—-work space, meetings, written materials—-and their work to be planned
- view their work as a helpful service to others, no matter what work they do

In Groups/On Teams

- prefer a collaborative, comfortable, harmonious work environment where people are included and valued, where there is open communication, and where contributions are recognized and appreciation is expressed
- create excitement and team spirit
- make things happen—-initiate, make proposals, spawn opportunities—-and can organize people for a project
- create opportunities for people to grow and develop

During Change

- propose and initiate change and are willing to try new approaches (sometimes can't leave well enough alone)
- are aware of and responsive to others' needs, and like change to benefit people
- can handle complex change situations, though they typically do so via a plan or structure
- may not have a good sense of their own energy limits and become susceptible to burn out

During Conflict

- have a need for and can create harmony, are tactful
- usually want to address conflicts immediately, may be worn down by long-term conflict even if it is peripheral to them
- prone to "take things personally", even when they aren't meant to be
- under stress, may criticize or blame, may adopt rigid stances or solutions, and may press to speed up the pace and take action even more quickly

Contributions

- creating an atmosphere and structures to help people reach their potential, and expect organizations to positively affect people, including their own employees
- serving as catalysts and motivators—-able to make things happen and keep them happening
- garnering resources to support efforts they believe in
- seeing things through to completion

May Be Experienced As

- decisive, coming to quick conclusions and *sometimes* as as deciding too quickly before considering sufficient options, impatient with others not as quick to act as they are
- eager and exuberant and *sometimes* as overwhelming others with enthusiasm, ideas, or requests
- promoters of people, values, and causes and *sometimes* as single-minded or inflexible regarding their own values or what is "best" for others
- having difficulty staying in the present, becoming overextended or overlooking their own needs

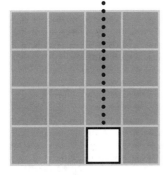

The Sixteen Types At Work

IS**T**Ps at work

Thinking

Sensing

Intuition

Feeling

What You Might Notice First

- have great curiosity about real things and want to know "why"
- have good grasp of details and a lot of information at their command, are tuned in to their surroundings
- are usually easy going, tolerant, and matter of fact
- are "get to the point" communicators

Work Style

- are active and hands on—like to have freedom to move about and a lot of direct sensory experiences
- want their efforts to have tangible and immediate results
- are pragmatic and expedient, want to take the most direct route to the goal (avoiding unnecessary steps and wasted motion), prefer minimal structure or standard procedures, and pride themselves on being able to get around the rules to get things done
- like to develop some skills to a high level of mastery (once developed, they may continue to hone them or move on to develop new ones)

In Groups/On Teams

- are tough-minded, analytical and critical, and independent-minded; they bring data for the group to use and help organize the information the team already has to make it useful
- quietly adapt to the needs of the moment
- are informal, ignoring or being impatient with with formal roles, titles, and official distinctions among people
- like and will be involved in creating fun, activity, and excitement

During Change

- want to jump in, roll up their sleeves and take action; they thrive in situations requiring rapid, in-the-moment responses, especially if there are apparently insurmountable hurdles
- may see planning as unnecessary and an impediment to action, and usually are not very interested in or don't see much use for theories or speculative models of change
- think realistically, and need to be convinced that change makes sense in order to go along with it
- are resilient, react to apparent failures by trying something else

During Conflict

- may offer information as an impartial basis for solving conflict, while they themselves desire to remain objective (and hence may be experienced by others as uncaring, not valuing people's feelings)
- are very good trouble shooters, may be at their best during difficult times or crises
- may let go of conflict for a while to see if it is resolved, but will take action if it persists
- under stress, may become irritated, quite task-oriented, overly sensitive, drag their feet, or withdraw

Contributions

- bringing accurate data to bear on team or organizational deliberations
- asking bedrock questions such as, "Why are we doing this?" or "Is this the most efficient way?"
- leading by doing—-showing the way, responding to windows of opportunity while the windows are still open, setting an example
- creating a sense of fun, playfulness, and adventure

May Be Experienced As

- making work playful and *sometimes* as not taking things seriously enough, possibly seeming to be amused by what others may consider serious matters
- disengaged observers, aloof, hard to get to know because they don't reveal much about themselves
- very responsive to the current situation and *sometimes* as so responsive to the immediate needs that new initiatives are undertaken while other work is still incomplete
- heavily engaged in and excited about non-work activities, interests, and hobbies

The Sixteen
Types
At Work

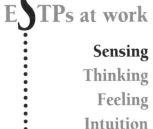

E**S**TPs at work

Sensing
Thinking
Feeling
Intuition

What You Might Notice First

- are energetic, action-oriented, outgoing, and restless—-want to have things happening and be involved
- are down-to-earth and expedient; they do what works but also like a challenge
- are troubleshooters and good in a crisis
- are curious and aware of things that others may overlook

Work Style

- size things up quickly and dive right in, are "hands-on" workers, may have intense bursts of energy to get something done "right now", and like seeing a task completed
- want to start doing it (rather than preparing a proposal or plan) and shape the work based on current experience, so they may begin with little planning and appear to "make it up" as they go along
- prefer minimal structure and procedures, and may stretch or ignore (and sometimes rebel against) rules to get the job done in the most straightforward, simple way
- like a variety of work and contact with a variety of people, like to learn new things, will seek out other activities or challenges if the work at hand is not sufficiently stimulating

In Groups/On Teams

- want to try something, not talk about what might be done (particularly if the discussion is prolonged or abstract)
- pay attention to and put energy into the issues, concerns, and tasks of the immediate present
- are persuasive, skilled at convincing others
- like to have fun at work; having fun is a motivator

During Change

- like and may be at their best during situations that require an immediate response, improvising, and thinking on one's feet; a crisis may call forth and highlight their leadership skills
- decide by doing so they may not know the best approach until it has been tried
- adapt readily to changing circumstances and are not reluctant to change courses in mid-stream, however, may also readily adapt to or accept what is and not see a need to change
- their action- or crisis-orientation may be experienced as stressful by others

During Conflict

- are good negotiators who are flexible, open minded, willing to compromise, and able see and bring together divergent views and the different sides to an issue
- willing to try new approach if the previous one didn't work, readily adopts others' ideas if they will work better
- may be less aware of or comfortable with the personal aspects of a conflict, so the solutions they propose may de-emphasize or overlook these elements
- under stress, may withdraw, become pessimistic, focus only on one option, or imagine "worst case" scenarios

Contributions

- resourcefulness—-making good use of what is at hand and being willing to jump in wherever needed
- create fun, liveliness, and activity, and introduce humor
- keep the team or organization reality-based
- flexibility, adaptability, and responsiveness

May Be Experienced As

- direct, straightforward communicators who tell it like it is and *sometimes* as quite frank, brusque, and unaware of or unresponsive to others' feelings and needs
- willing to take risks and wanting the team or organization to do the same
- action-oriented and *sometimes* as so inclined to act that they overlook the long term implications and put energy into ideas that are not well thought out
- not consistent at follow through, "winging it", "last minute", or putting off tasks deemed unimportant

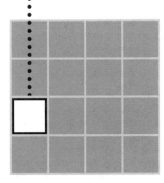

The Sixteen Types At Work

I**N**FJs at work

Intuition
Feeling
Thinking
Sensing

What You Might Notice First

- are warm, cooperative, trusting, sensitive, tactful, and easy to get along with (though they may also keep their distance or seem aloof at first)
- have good communication skills, are persuasive, and are good listeners
- are dependable and persistent; they do what they agree to do and meet obligations
- seem to "have their act together"

Work Style

- prefer a supportive environment that is friendly and non-competitive and where harmony and praise are common
- see work as a mission or service — want work to make a difference for others and want to grow through their work
- like variety and opportunities to be creative, and dream up new approaches to the routine
- value independence and autonomy, and want to organize their own time, effort, and work environment

In Groups/On Teams

- are imaginative, have or generate ideas (though ideas may have to be drawn out of them), are comfortable with abstraction and complexity, and can synthesize multiple perspectives or diverse information
- encourage and empower others, want and give appreciation and affirmation, seek to create cohesion
- prefer to have both organization and structure <u>and</u> concern for people and humane values; want the team to organize itself around vision and values
- are good at working on teams, though too much of a group can fatigue or overload them

During Change

- may experience tension between being too oriented toward newness and change and honoring traditions and what has proven to be comfortable for people
- look for and may be aware of significance in events that others may miss or deem unimportant
- use symbols and metaphors to visualize and talk about change
- may withdraw if their ideas are not accepted or their values are not respected

During Conflict

- prize and strive for harmony, take a facilitative approach
- are often peacemakers and mediators who know how to resolve difficulties and are able to find some good in a painful situation
- may take on and/or internalize others' concerns
- under stress, may want to be alone, may make absolute statements and speak harshly of themselves or others, and/or may become distracted and give considerable energy to a low priority task

Contributions

- strong and idealistic belief in people and in what they can accomplish, and encouragement of others to maximize their abilities and potential
- visionary—-advocating their visions, values, and ideals
- insight into people, sometimes being aware of others' needs before others themselves are
- promoting integrity and the alignment of values and actions for individuals, groups and organizations—-calling upon organizations to "walk their talk"

May Be Experienced As

- having strong convictions, inner vision and lofty goals and *sometimes* as being single-minded and inflexible about how things ought to be
- indirect and private, so they may be hard to get to know
- self-critical, hard on themselves, and "perfectionistic"
- liking to dig into things deeply and *sometimes* as tending to exhaustive exploration or over-analysis

The Sixteen Types At Work

ESFPs at work

Sensing

Feeling

Thinking

Intuition

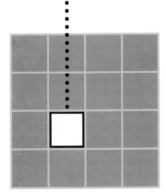

What You Might Notice First

- enthusiastic and energetic, warm and joyful, optimistic and uplifting, accepting of others
- like to be where the people and the action are (right in the middle of things), involved, gregarious, and sociable
- communicative, often have good people skills, and take a sympathetic approach to others
- observant, pay attention to what is going on in their environment

Work Style

- enjoy being with others, like to work with a variety of people and challenges, and want the job to be fun
- see and put themselves in a helping role and like to feel personally involved in their work
- have an involved, hands-on work style; trust more and learn best from direct experience (try it first, read the instructions if stuck)
- like freedom to be active and prefer little structure

In Groups/On Teams

- bring a sense of unity to the team, work to create an environment where people feel valued and in on things, and encourage others or spur them on
- share about themselves and their life's experiences, and can be a catalyst for others to do same
- attend to the people and processes before the task; value cooperative, harmonious relationships where people are regarded as equals
- flexible and adaptable, favor altering plans to account for team or individual needs as they arise

During Change

- prefer change that is directed toward specific, people-oriented goals—with lots of encouragement and support to reach those goals
- are comfortable moving into a hectic situation and helping others/the team through a crisis, often come through difficult situations with flying colors
- practical and realistic problem solvers who respond and improvise according to the needs of the moment
- more prone to act than to plan or systematically consider the alternatives

During Conflict

- value unity and agreement, and may find conflict among people unsettling
- tactful, not confrontational—may withhold "constructive criticism" even when providing it would be helpful
- can often bring a sense of ease to a tense situation
- under stress, may be uncharacteristically pessimistic, negative, or doubt themselves (though they may not show these reactions overtly)

Contributions

- concern for people—help keep the focus on the needs of the people being served (e.g., customer, patient, student)
- bring and help create excitement, optimism, and fun
- ability to pay attention to and keep track of numerous things at the same time
- being open about themselves and their concerns (what you see is what you get), and encouraging others to be the same

May Be Experienced As

- very aware of others' needs and *sometimes* as wearing themselves out trying to meet those needs
- liking everything to be fun and *sometimes* as too light hearted
- quite responsive to immediate demands and *sometimes* as so adaptable that they may not see the need for making plans, may become diverted and leave things unfinished, or may deviate from established routines
- high energy and giving others a lot of personal attention and *sometimes* as overpowering or putting others off with the attention they give

The Sixteen Types At Work

I**N**TJs at work

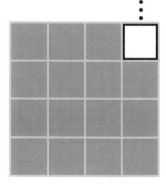

Intuition

Thinking

Feeling

Sensing

What You Might Notice First

- are serious and confident
- are independent, may seem cool, impersonal, and distant, and don't communicate much
- are inquisitive and skeptical, raise questions about everything (e.g., organizational mission, current goals, why we've been organized into teams)
- have ideas in mind so they propose solutions and give advice (and may be blunt in doing so)

Work Style

- are comfortable working alone and like to have their own work space
- do their best work when they have a grasp of the big picture and the underlying principles, want to understand something before trying it, and once they understand it they may not be interested in implementation
- function autonomously, often want and provide little feedback or supervision, and may take action without informing or consulting others
- highly value competence in self and others, and like to continue to learn and expand their capabilities

In Groups/On Teams

- are not naturally drawn to teams and may appear uninvolved or uncommitted
- boil much of the group's discussion and deliberation down to essential points or issues
- are intellectually playful, but otherwise earnest
- may not value or be comfortable with the relationship-building aspects of working together (e.g., "small talk", creating a warm environment)

During Change

- project calm and often provide a stabilizing influence
- see change as a means to improve, to address weaknesses and problems in systems, or to achieve specific organizational outcomes; may be less enthusiastic about personal change
- are not particularly responsive to—-and may deliberately resist—-external pressures (e.g, "This is the latest approach" or "All the other departments are doing it")
- want to know "why", and take a rational, systematic approach to change, even to the human factors involved

During Conflict

- want to analyze all components, including "irrational" aspects to look for patterns or cause and effect relationships
- may avoid or withdraw unless the conflict is an obstacle to accomplishing something important to them
- sometimes cause conflict without being aware that they are (e.g., may spark discussions and arguments that others experience as conflict, or may offer suggestions for improvement that others take as personal criticisms)
- under stress, may feel immobilized, have irrational/emotional reactions, or give sudden priority to seemingly insignificant activities or events

Contributions

- generate and promote "vision", and take a long-range view of the consequences of today's deliberations
- able to see things from a new perspective, providing original ideas or insights and synthesizing complex information or diverse perspectives
- drive and readiness to create and improve systems
- advocate focusing energy and resources on activities central to accomplishing the mission

May Be Experienced As

- persevering and determined and *sometimes* as so confident their position is right that they stubbornly hang on to ideas and visions too long
- competent and self-assured and *sometimes* as seeming to regard themselves as superior to others
- providing relatively little information, presuming that what is perfectly clear to them is also clear to others
- having demanding standards, and *sometimes* as critical of self and others when standards aren't met

The Sixteen Types At Work

E**N**TPs at work

Intuition
Thinking
Feeling
Sensing

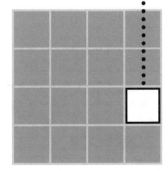

What You Might Notice First
- generate and are engaged by ideas and possibilities, inventive, make connections quickly
- have lots going on, are lively, contribute to a highly charged environment
- approach most things—and people—logically and analytically
- are outgoing, articulate, assertive, and confident in their ideas and abilities

Work Style
- like variety and activity in work, people, and methods; are energized and stimulated by new problems and challenges; get involved with others; not inclined to sit still
- do things in novel or non-standard ways, and may look for ways to go around or outwit the system
- value competence in self and others—want to work with others whom they regard as competent, and seek new challenges and opportunities to test or expand their abilities; do not like and may resist close supervision
- may move ahead without a complete plan, agenda, or all necessary materials

In Groups/On Teams
- have enthusiastic, entrepreneurial characters and champion ideas, can win support of and motivate others, and like their own ideas and contributions to be recognized
- are comfortable with and begin with the big picture (abstract, future possibilities) and are less interested in the specifics of implementation; can see multiple points of view and may frustrate others by seeming to change their minds as new information or options emerge
- seek to create a stimulating environment, want work to be playful and fun, and often engage in intellectual play
- like to communicate directly and straightforwardly, readily offer suggestions for improvement or provide critiques

During Change
- energized by, create, and stir up change; like to start new things
- see or generate many options for how change could occur, can almost always see another possibility
- are adaptive and go with the flow
- are comfortable beginning with a concept or model—what may seem like just a rough idea to others—and creating whatever is needed as they go along

During Conflict
- want to use analysis and principles to resolve conflict and may take an objective, non-personal approach to people
- want to talk about the conflict, though they are not usually bothered by (and may be stimulated by) intellectual give and take or debate
- able to see all sides and points of view
- under stress, may become inappropriately and extremely focused on or distracted by a few specifics, and may have bursts of misdirected energy

Contributions
- want to keep themselves and the team or organization on the cutting edge and pushing boundaries via creativity, risk taking, and exploring whatever is new
- well-developed, though sometimes irreverent, sense of humor
- ability to synthesize a variety of sometimes disparate perspectives and information into a new whole
- the desire, persistence, and resourcefulness to solve problems and make things happen

May Be Experienced As
- high energy and tireless and *sometimes* as having too many activities going on at once, overwhelming or distracting others with possibilities and complexity
- lacking closure or follow through—pushing deadlines and seeming to be pushed for time
- competitive, arguing for the fun of it and *sometimes* as wanting to be "one up"
- having high expectations and *sometimes* as impatient and critical of self and others when standards are not met

The Sixteen Types At Work

I**S**FJs at work

Sensing
Feeling
Thinking
Intuition

What You Might Notice First

- are warm, friendly, good-natured, unassuming, sensitive to others, and good listeners; yet may also be constrained and not communicate a lot, especially about themselves
- are hard working, steady, and dependable, and they have a strong sense of responsibility and duty
- are down-to-earth, practical, and realistic; they follow procedures and respect traditions and the way things are done
- are organized and good at organizing both people and things

Work Style

- prefer to plan the work and be prepared for the snares and obstacles that might be encountered, and are most comfortable getting organized before beginning a project
- are most drawn to work that is helpful and provides a tangible service to others
- prefer to work on one thing at a time, giving attention to one person or project without interruption
- want to know specifically what is expected of them

In Groups/On Teams

- seek to create a non-threatening, supportive environment; generally they are concerned and involved group members who need time to get to know others and begin to build solid working relationships
- favor establishing clear goals, objectives, schedules, milestones, etc., and are comfortable working within hierarchical structures
- expect everyone to do their share and pull their own weight (ISFJ's themselves often do more than their share)
- do best when they are recognized for their contributions (especially when many of their accomplishments are less conspicuous)

During Change

- foster change that addresses people's unmet needs and helps them to develop and become "better persons"
- often respect experience and tradition and therefore prefer gradual change and may take a "don't rock the boat" stance
- value fairness and want change to be fair and have a similar impact on all
- bring a sense of stability by creating structure and order; do best when change can be well-planned

During Conflict

- prefer and work best when there is harmony, support, and affirmation (lack of harmony—such as office feuds—can be upsetting and throw them off track); may use gentle humor to try to create harmony
- tactful, kind, gentle, considerate, and aware of and responsive to what others are experiencing and feeling; may use the "I've been there technique" to help others resolve conflict
- very sensitive and may take negative feedback and "constructive criticism" personally
- under stress, may be uncharacteristically pessimistic and/or disorganized

Contributions

- focus on getting the job done and creating a supportive, positive environment
- show strong loyalty to the organization
- value follow through and focus individual or group efforts on achieving what they set out to do; they themselves work quietly, sometimes unnoticed, to make sure that things run smoothly
- bring stability, calm, organization and structure to projects or departments/teams

May Be Experienced As

- good with detail, patient, thorough and *sometimes* as "picky" about details, too structured, not spontaneous
- serious, deep and reserved, and *sometimes* as hard to read, taking longer to get to know
- communicating indirectly, "beating around the bush"
- concerned that things go well and *sometimes* as overly concerned "worriers"

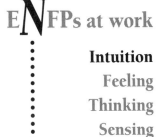

E**N**FPs at work

Intuition
Feeling
Thinking
Sensing

What You Might Notice First

- are lively and often full of excitement, stimulate activity, and get others excited
- generate a lot of ideas and options; seem to be surrounded by possibilities; are expansive and imaginative
- are expressive, articulate, and communicate a lot
- are people-oriented—engaging and optimistic

Work Style

- are most drawn to work that has meaning and value for them and which fosters human growth
- are cooperative and are natural networkers who do best when they have contact with/stimulation from others (they don't usually like working alone)
- work from inspiration, not a plan, and like to develop new approaches and create new things; are flexible and prefer not to have routines, a lot of structure, or tight schedules; work in bursts of energy
- like challenges and a variety of people and tasks, want to continue to learn and develop

In Groups/On Teams

- are catalysts, initiators, and motivators who get things going, and are energized by starting something new
- attend to the "people" and group process aspects of the team, notice and encourage the gifts in others, want and give recognition, and work to develop and maintain harmonious, inclusive relationships
- are fun loving, bring and stimulate energy and gusto
- are adaptable and dexterous—willing to jump in wherever needed (without being particularly concerned about "authorship" or who gets credit)

During Change

- are natural change agents who are energized and captivated by change, and often have a "let's give it a try/go with the flow" outlook (especially when change supports their overall vision)
- place high priority on changes which make things better for people, including themselves and their team members
- can brainstorm numerous possibilities
- are motivated to change themselves in response to feedback from someone they trust, or by becoming aware of how their behavior affects or is perceived by others

During Conflict

- value interpersonal harmony, emphasize areas of accord and unity, and de-emphasize points of contention
- are peacemakers and accommodators who may be asked to play—or put themselves in—the role of conciliator
- want to consider and incorporate everyone's viewpoint, and can help move the team toward consensus
- under stress, may be direct or confrontational, compulsive about small tasks and details, or take a rigid stance

Contributions

- visionary and idealistic, want the organization, team, and individuals to pursue the vision and make a difference for people
- willing to try new things and take risks, impart a sense of adventure
- have a strong people orientation—people are drawn to them and they can draw people out and fire them up
- promote establishing and adhering to team or organizational values

May Be Experienced As

- visionary dreamers and *sometimes* as appearing to lack direction and focus
- having a lot going on and *sometimes* as being over-committed ("having too many balls in the air"), moving from one project or cause to another when a more intriguing possibility arises, leaving others to follow through or wonder what happened to the previous project or cause
- generating a lot of alternatives and *sometimes* as having difficulty deciding among all the alternatives they generate so they may seem to "waffle" or appear "wishy washy"
- disarming, having ready and plausible explanations for most occurrences

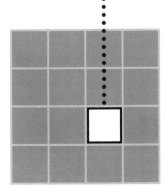

The Sixteen Types At Work

ISTJs at work

Sensing
Thinking
Feeling
Intuition

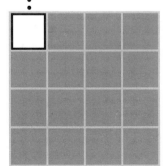

What You Might Notice First

- are organized, dependable, persistent, and do what's sensible
- are quiet and less engaged with others so they may seem impersonal or detached
- have a strong sense of duty and responsibility; they do not waste time, money, or other resources, and they follow procedures and rules that have a logical purpose (and expect others to do the same)
- are attentive to details and bring a vast array of facts and data to bear on their work

Work Style

- are methodical, like to have as much information as possible about the task before proceeding, plan their work, and strive to stick to the plan (usually they are not comfortable figuring it out as they go along)
- like clear responsibilities and rewards, tangible and measurable objectives, well-defined tasks, and specific instructions
- use established techniques to complete tasks, work within existing frameworks, and get job done right and on time
- prefer to work on one thing at a time and not to be pulled in too many directions, able to alone, and don't like interruptions

In Groups/On Teams

- are often relied on for accurate information (e.g., up-to-date figures, complete notes or minutes)
- are task-oriented so their first concern is to get the work done and they may be less attentive to the group's process and the "goings on" of the team (which may seem to take too much energy from the work)
- like a clear structure (or chain of command), and want the team to have clear objectives, schedules and deadlines
- want the team to be moving toward its objectives and may be impatient with protracted deliberations and mulling over multiple options

During Change

- bring realism and have a clear notion of what seems feasible
- are stabilizers who are cautious and naturally conservative
- are most comfortable with and supportive of incremental change that preserves and builds on what has been shown to work
- because of these views, may be experienced as resistant to change

During Conflict

- project calm—-often do not appear bothered by conflicts which are upsetting others (though they may have internalized them)—-and propose sensible, matter-of-fact solutions
- try to remain rational, reasonable, and objective about everything including emotions; not necessarily comfortable with emotions and may regard it as inappropriate to bring them into workplace deliberations and issues
- seek the support of someone with whom they are close to confide in
- under stress, may be particularly pessimistic, see only "worst case" possibilities, and start to doubt themselves

Contributions

- bring the historical perspective, may be the team or organizational memory or historian
- emphasize productivity and efficiency—-getting the job done while making good use of resources
- strong allegiance to individuals and organizations
- precision, objectivity, and thoroughness

May Be Experienced As

- determined—-establishing objectives and doing what it takes to reach them—-and *sometimes* as so determined that *they seem set in their ways, stubborn, and not open to considering other alternatives*
- hard working and productive and *sometimes as too serious and proper*
- noticing and pointing out things which are inconsistent with standard practices or seeming to be "unfair"
- hard to get to know, removed

Types and Work

Do different types of people choose different kinds of work? When you are in the accounting department how likely is it that you are interacting with types different from those you will encounter in human resources? You can see for yourself in the next few pages.

The Center for Applications of Psychological Type has a large collection of data on the types of people who tend to be found in various work roles and professions. This section includes type tables showing the type breakdowns in roles and professions common to many organizations. For the purpose of comparison, a type table (called "Total Form G Databank") representing the breakdown of type in a large (but not random) sample of the general population is also included.

The "type table" is a standard way to summarize and report information about a particular group. The table itself shows the percent of the total group identifying with each of the 16 types. For example, on page 33, the data in the upper left shows that 22.09% in this sample of 824 accountants belong to the ISTJ group, and in the lower right it shows 6.31% in the ENTJ group.

The information to the right of the type table includes the percents of various combinations of preferences that occur in the group. Again, using the accountants as an example, we see at the top of the right hand column that 44.17% are extraverted and, going down to the third grouping, that 44.54% have ST preferences and 12.74% have preferences for NF.

Two interesting things are often evident when we have a fairly large sample of people from a particular professional group or work role. First, all 16 types are usually represented, though not in equal proportion. Second, the groups which occur most and least frequently are predictable from type theory. With the accountants, the percents range from 1.70% for ESFP to 22.09% for ISTJ. Slightly over 37% of the whole group come from just two types—ISTJ and ESTJ—known to pay attention to detail, to prefer working with objective data and decision rules, and to work best in a deliberate and structured fashion.

On the next six pages you will find type tables for groups you may work with—managers and supervisors, executive secretaries, marketing personnel, accountants, and information specialists—-as well as one representing CAPT's data base. Many other groups are included in the CAPT *Atlas of Type Tables* (see the Helpful Resources section for a complete citation).

Estimated Frequencies of the Types in the United States Population

Total				
E 45–53%	**ISTJ** 11–14%	**ISFJ** 9–14%	**INFJ** 1–3%	**INTJ** 2–4%
I 47–55%				
S 66–74%	**ISTP** 4–6%	**ISFP** 5–9%	**INFP** 4–5%	**INTP** 3–5%
N 26–34%				
T 40–50%				
F 50–60%	**ESTP** 4–5%	**ESFP** 4–9%	**ENFP** 6–8%	**ENTP** 2–5%
J 54–60%				
P 40–46%	**ESTJ** 8–12%	**ESFJ** 9–13%	**ENFJ** 2–5%	**ENTJ** 2–5%

Source: *Estimated Frequencies of the Types in the United States Population* developed by Charles R. Martin, Ph.D. Revised by Allen L. Hammer, Ph.D., based on more recent analyses conducted by Glenn Grannade. Gainesville, FL: Center for Applications of Psychological Type, Inc., 2003.

Managers, Administrators, and Supervisors

N = 4808

Sensing		Intuition	
Thinking	Feeling	Feeling	Thinking

ISTJ	ISFJ	INFJ	INTJ
N = 935	N = 261	N = 124	N = 392
% = 19.45	% = 5.43	% = 2.58	% = 8.15
■■■■■■■■■ ■■■■■■■■■ ■■■■	■■■■■	■■■	■■■■■■■■

Judgment — Introversion

ISTP	ISFP	INFP	INTP
N = 175	N = 80	N = 130	N = 280
% = 3.64	% = 1.66	% = 2.70	% = 5.82
■■■■	■■	■■■	■■■■■■

Perception

ESTP	ESFP	ENFP	ENTP
N = 158	N = 93	N = 203	N = 285
% = 3.29	% = 1.93	% = 4.22	% = 5.93
■■■	■■	■■■■	■■■■■■

Perception — Extraversion

ESTJ	ESFJ	ENFJ	ENTJ
N = 786	N = 218	N = 177	N = 511
% = 16.35	% = 4.53	% = 3.68	% = 10.63
■■■■■■■■ ■■■■■■■■	■■■■■	■■■■	■■■■■■■■■■ ■■■

Judgment

	N	%
E	2431	50.56
I	2377	49.44
S	2706	56.28
N	2102	43.72
T	3522	73.25
F	1286	26.75
J	3404	70.80
P	1404	29.20
I J	1712	35.61
I P	665	13.83
E P	739	15.37
E J	1692	35.19
S T	2054	42.72
S F	652	13.56
N F	634	13.19
N T	1468	30.53
S J	2200	45.76
S P	506	10.52
N P	898	18.68
N J	1204	25.04
T J	2624	54.58
T P	898	18.68
F P	506	10.52
F J	780	16.22
I N	926	19.26
E N	1176	24.46
I S	1451	30.18
E S	1255	26.10
E T	1740	36.19
E F	691	14.37
I F	595	12.38
I T	1782	37.06
S dom	1447	30.10
N dom	1004	20.88
T dom	1752	36.44
F dom	605	12.58

Note: ■ = 1% of sample

Source: Gerald P. Macdaid, CAPT Data Bank, 1997,
Center for Applications of Psychological Type, Inc.

Secretaries and Administrative Assistants

N = 2299

	Sensing		Intuition	
	Thinking	**Feeling**	**Feeling**	**Thinking**

ISTJ	**ISFJ**	**INFJ**	**INTJ**
N = 272	N = 402	N = 109	N = 62
% = 11.83	% = 17.49	% = 4.74	% = 2.70
■■■■■■■■■■ ■■■■	■■■■■■■■■■■ ■■■■■■■■■ ■	■■■■■	■■■

ISTP	**ISFP**	**INFP**	**INTP**
N = 61	N = 124	N = 134	N = 49
% = 2.65	% = 5.39	% = 5.83	% = 2.13
■■■	■■■■■	■■■■■■	■■

ESTP	**ESFP**	**ENFP**	**ENTP**
N = 39	N = 95	N = 169	N = 65
% = 1.70	% = 4.13	% = 7.35	% = 2.83
■■	■■■■	■■■■■■■	■■■

ESTJ	**ESFJ**	**ENFJ**	**ENTJ**
N = 208	N = 305	N = 135	N = 70
% = 9.05	% = 13.27	% = 5.87	% = 3.04
■■■■■■■■■ ■	■■■■■■■■■■ ■■■■■	■■■■■■	■■■

Right side labels: Introversion — Judgment / Perception; Extraversion — Perception / Judgment

	N	%
E	1086	47.24
I	1213	52.76
S	1506	65.51
N	793	34.49
T	826	35.93
F	1473	64.07
J	1563	67.99
P	736	32.01
I J	845	36.76
I P	368	16.01
E P	368	16.01
E J	718	31.23
S T	580	25.23
S F	926	40.28
N F	547	23.79
N T	246	10.70
S J	1187	51.63
S P	319	13.88
N P	417	18.14
N J	376	16.35
T J	612	26.62
T P	214	9.31
F P	522	22.71
F J	951	41.37
I N	354	15.40
E N	439	19.10
I S	859	37.36
E S	647	28.14
E T	382	16.62
E F	704	30.62
I F	769	33.45
I T	444	19.31
S dom	808	35.15
N dom	405	17.62
T dom	388	16.88
F dom	698	30.36

Note: ■ = 1% of sample

Source: Gerald P. Macdaid, CAPT Data Bank, 1997,
Center for Applications of Psychological Type, Inc.

Marketing Personnel

N = 448

	Sensing		Intuition	
	Thinking	Feeling	Feeling	Thinking

ISTJ	ISFJ	INFJ	INTJ
N = 36	N = 9	N = 17	N = 35
% = 8.04	% = 2.01	% = 3.79	% = 7.81
■■■■■■■■	■■	■■■■	■■■■■■■■

ISTP	ISFP	INFP	INTP
N = 7	N = 3	N = 10	N = 29
% = 1.56	% = 0.67	% = 2.23	% = 6.47
■■	■	■■■	■■■■■■

ESTP	ESFP	ENFP	ENTP
N = 17	N = 7	N = 34	N = 41
% = 3.79	% = 1.56	% = 7.59	% = 9.15
■■■■	■■	■■■■■■■■	■■■■■■■■■ ■

ESTJ	ESFJ	ENFJ	ENTJ
N = 85	N = 21	N = 26	N = 71
% = 18.97	% = 4.69	% = 5.80	% = 15.85
■■■■■■■■ ■■■■■■■■ ■■■	■■■■■	■■■■■■■	■■■■■■■■■ ■■■■■■■■

Judgment — Introversion (Judgment) / Perception — Introversion
Perception — Extraversion / Judgment — Extraversion

	N	%
E	302	67.41
I	146	32.59
S	185	41.29
N	263	58.71
T	321	71.65
F	127	28.35
J	300	66.96
P	148	33.04
I J	97	21.65
I P	49	10.94
E P	99	22.10
E J	203	45.31
S T	145	32.37
S F	40	8.93
N F	87	19.42
N T	176	39.29
S J	151	33.71
S P	34	7.59
N P	114	25.45
N J	149	33.26
T J	227	50.67
T P	94	20.98
F P	54	12.05
F J	73	16.29
I N	91	20.31
E N	172	38.39
I S	55	12.28
E S	130	29.02
E T	214	47.77
E F	88	19.64
I F	39	8.71
I T	107	23.88
S dom	69	15.40
N dom	127	28.35
T dom	192	42.86
F dom	60	13.39

Note: ■ = 1% of sample

Source: Gerald P. Macdaid, CAPT Data Bank, 1997,
Center for Applications of Psychological Type, Inc.

Accountants

N = 824

	Sensing		Intuition	
	Thinking	**Feeling**	**Feeling**	**Thinking**

ISTJ	ISFJ	INFJ	INTJ
N = 182	N = 70	N = 19	N = 46
% = 22.09	% = 8.50	% = 2.31	% = 5.58
■■■■■■■■ ■■■■■■■■ ■■■■■■	■■■■■■■■■	■■	■■■■■■

ISTP	ISFP	INFP	INTP
N = 42	N = 36	N = 24	N = 41
% = 5.10	% = 4.37	% = 2.91	% = 4.98
■■■■■	■■■■	■■■	■■■■■

ESTP	ESFP	ENFP	ENTP
N = 20	N = 14	N = 28	N = 39
% = 2.43	% = 1.70	% = 3.40	% = 4.73
■■	■■	■■■	■■■■■

ESTJ	ESFJ	ENFJ	ENTJ
N = 123	N = 54	N = 34	N = 52
% = 14.93	% = 6.55	% = 4.13	% = 6.31
■■■■■■■■■ ■■■■■■■	■■■■■■■■■	■■■■	■■■■■■

Judgment — Introversion — Perception
Perception — Extraversion — Judgment

	N	%
E	364	44.17
I	460	55.83
S	541	65.66
N	283	34.34
T	545	66.14
F	279	33.86
J	580	70.39
p	244	29.61
I J	317	38.47
I P	143	17.35
E P	101	12.26
E J	263	31.92
S T	367	44.54
S F	174	21.12
N F	105	12.74
N T	178	21.60
S J	429	52.06
S P	112	13.59
N P	132	16.02
N J	151	18.33
T J	403	48.91
T P	142	17.23
F P	102	12.38
F J	177	21.48
I N	130	15.78
E N	153	18.57
I S	330	40.05
E S	211	25.61
E T	234	28.40
E F	130	15.78
I F	149	18.08
I T	311	37.74
S dom	286	34.71
N dom	132	16.02
T dom	258	31.31
F dom	148	17.96

Note: ■ = 1% of sample

Source: Gerald P. Macdaid, CAPT Data Bank, 1997,
Center for Applications of Psychological Type, Inc.

Human Resource Workers

N = 380

	Sensing		Intuition				N	%
	Thinking	**Feeling**	**Feeling**	**Thinking**				
	ISTJ N = 38 % = 10.00	**ISFJ** N = 15 % =3.95	**INFJ** N = 9 % = 2.37	**INTJ** N = 33 % = 8.68	Judgment / Introversion	E	223	58.68
						I	157	41.32
						S	146	38.42
						N	234	61.58
						T	231	60.79
						F	149	39.21
						J	233	61.32
						P	147	38.68
	ISTP N = 7 % = 1.84	**ISFP** N = 3 % = 0.79	**INFP** N = 25 % = 6.58	**INTP** N = 27 % = 7.11	Perception	I J	95	25.00
						I P	62	16.32
						E P	85	22.37
						E J	138	36.32
						S T	95	25.00
						S F	51	13.42
						N F	98	25.79
						N T	136	35.79
	ESTP N = 5 % = 1.32	**ESFP** N = 11 % =2.89	**ENFP** N = 36 % = 9.47	**ENTP** N = 33 % = 8.68	Perception / Extraversion	S J	120	31.58
						S P	26	6.84
						N P	121	31.84
						N J	113	29.74
						T J	159	41.84
						T P	72	18.95
						F P	75	19.74
						F J	74	19.47
	ESTJ N = 45 % = 11.84	**ESFJ** N = 22 % =5.79	**ENFJ** N = 28 % = 7.37	**ENTJ** N = 43 % = 11.32	Judgment	I N	94	24.74
						E N	140	36.84
						I S	63	16.58
						E S	83	21.84
						E T	126	33.16
						E F	97	25.53
						I F	52	13.68
						I T	105	27.63
						S dom	69	18.16
						N dom	111	29.21
						T dom	122	32.11
						F dom	78	20.53

Note: ■ = 1% of sample

Source: Gerald P. Macdaid, CAPT Data Bank, 1997,
Center for Applications of Psychological Type, Inc.

Putting Type to Work

For some people, just learning about type theory and the 16 types is interesting, even fascinating, in and of itself. For others, it doesn't become interesting until they see how it can be put to use. "So what?" is the question on their minds. Some of the "so whats" of type at work are briefly considered here.

Our own psychological type and the types of our co-workers can be a major influence on how we behave and what we consider important in many facets of everyday workplace interactions and activities, including

- our communication styles
- our approaches to decision making and problem solving
- our work styles
- what we find motivating and rewarding
- giving and receiving feedback
- participation on a team
- responding to conflict
- our views of the "ideal"—the ideal boss, job, co-worker, team, organization
- supervisory, management, and leadership styles
- how we approach the particular kind of work we do
- what we find stressful and how we respond to stress
- how we like our work space arranged and decorated
- time management and organizing
- our teaching and learning styles when we are involved in education and training
- the culture of the organizations we work in.

Six of these elements—how psychological type can affect our responses to conflict, the functioning on a team, our work style, our approaches to problem solving and decision making, our postures toward change, and our preferred ways to communicate—are the focus of this section.

Of course, our type preferences are only one of the factors influencing our behavior at work. Our own education and training, the specific kind of work we do, the nature of the business or service provided, and the culture of the organization are among the many other influences. Type is an important ingredient, but certainly not the only one.

Responding to Conflict

People experience conflict over a variety of things—goals, roles, territory, methods, values, styles, facts. From the perspective of type, there are three other factors that may enter into dealing with conflict. People with different type preferences may differ about

- whether there is a conflict,
- if anything should be done about it, and
- what should be done.

Extraverts and Introverts

Extraverts and introverts may differ about *how to approach* a conflict.

Extraverts usually prefer to talk about ("process", "deal with", "confront") conflicts, and may want to do so while the conflict is fresh, sometimes even while it is still going on. "Talk first and reflect on it afterwards" might well be their watchword. Introverts usually prefer to take time to think about it, and they may pull back to ponder, seeming to withdraw, without letting others know that's what they're doing. They will be more comfortable talking about it after they've had a chance to reflect on it.

These tendencies—and the tendencies associated with the other MBTI preferences—can create

Putting Type to Work

challenges whether the participants in a conflict have different preferences or they share the same ones.

Here are some brief illustrations of how extraversion and introversion can affect our responses to conflict.

- Extraverts in conflict with one another may need to find a way they both can feel heard. In particularly tense or difficult situations, a "cooling off period" which provides some time to reflect and analyze may be advisable.
- Two introverts may be challenged to make sure they actually address the conflict together. They may pull back to reflect on it but not come back together and tell one another what they were thinking about.
- An introvert and an extravert may need to agree on a particular time to come together—a time that gives the introvert an opportunity to reflect and also allows the extravert to feel as though the conflict will be addressed while it is relatively fresh and not be put on hold too long.

Sensing Types and Intuitive Types

Sensing types and intuitive types may differ about the *facts and what they mean*. Sensing types tend to focus first on the details of the current situation, and having a complete and accurate rendering of the specifics is vital. Since "the facts speak for themselves", initially it is less important to them to explore the underlying meaning of the conflict.

Focusing at first on trends or patterns, intuitive types are prone to generalize about or interpret the events. They want to understand the significance of what has happened. Initially it is less important that all the specifics be taken into account, so they may seem to skip over some of the facts or treat them cavalierly.

Here are some brief illustrations of how sensing and intuition can affect our responses to conflict.

- If they happen to have different versions of the facts, a challenge for sensing types in conflict with one another could be finding a common description of what happened. Because they naturally tend to pay attention to the trees before seeing the forest, they may need to be deliberate about identifying recurrent themes or issues (otherwise they find themselves repeatedly having to address similar conflicts).
- Naturally interested in reaching general conclusions and inferring the overall meaning, two intuitive types may need to make sure they have enough information about the reality of what happened to support their views and conclusions. Jointly writing down (e.g., on a flip chart) what they recall may help. They might also want to consider checking their perceptions out with others who are knowledgeable.
- When a sensing type and an intuitive type have conflict, it may be helpful for them to agree on a process that will encompass both parties' preferred kind of information—possibly beginning by clarifying each person's view of what took place and then moving on to search for recurring issues or themes and to generate alternative courses of action.

Thinking Types and Feeling Types

Thinking types and feeling types may differ on what to take into consideration in crafting a workable solution. People with a preference for thinking typically act because something is logical or "makes sense". They try to remain objective, keeping what they regard as the logical, impartial issues separate from the subjective, feeling issues. They may maintain that feeling issues should not be part of discussions at work or that conflict should be accepted as normal in the workplace. Analytical, they may approach conflict, even an interpersonal one, as they would any other problem. Sometimes they are not aware that an issue causing conflict for others has arisen and they may wonder "what all the fuss is about".

Those with a preference for feeling typically want to select a course of action based on how it will

Putting Type to Work

affect people or because it "feels right". Feeling types are often the first ones aware of a conflict and may want to address it in order to have the sense of harmony they need to do their best work. They view the consideration of feeling issues not only as appropriate at work, but crucial to developing a healthy, productive environment.

Here are some brief illustrations of how thinking and feeling can affect our responses to conflict.

- Two thinking types with conflict are likely to devise logical and sensible solutions, but may not give sufficient consideration to how people—including themselves—will be affected. As they are delineating the factors to consider (perhaps going through a mental or actual checklist), those who prefer thinking may well want to add "effect on people" to their list. (Collecting apparently objective data about subjective factors via employee surveys is another way for thinking types to include more people-oriented concerns.)

- Prizing harmonious relationships, two feeling types searching for common ground may de-emphasize their issues or differences and may need to be direct and assertive about their own viewpoints and needs. They may also benefit by checking to see that they have given sufficient weight to objective, business-oriented factors (e.g., by utilizing information such as financial statements or marketing forecasts, or by consulting with others who normally take the "bottom line" perspective).

- Efforts to deal with conflicts involving those with a preference for thinking and those with a preference for feeling sometimes introduce yet another thing to be in conflict about—the process of interacting with one another. Those preferring thinking often communicate directly, perhaps bluntly, and may seem to give insufficient weight to feeling concerns. To those who prefer feeling, this approach may well just provide further indication that the thinking types "don't get it".

In turn, those who prefer feeling may begin with and emphasize points the parties have in common rather than raising the conflict itself. Thinking types may interpret this to mean that conflict is not a priority because it seems as though there is more agreement than disagreement and that a forceful case is not being made for addressing it (i.e., "what's the big deal").

Two approaches can be helpful here. First, each person can adjust their normal communication style and attend to and use one another's vocabulary when appropriate. Checking back to see if the other feels "heard" would also be good. Doing these things could help avoid having the interaction itself become another point of contention.

Second, similar to the strategy suggested when there is an S-N difference, the participants can adopt an approach that assures both kinds of factors—objective and subjective—will be given due consideration in reaching a resolution. These concerns and criteria might be listed side-by-side on a flip chart and checked off once they have been addressed.

Judging types and Perceiving types

Judging types and perceiving types may disagree about how quickly an agreement should be reached. As people who prefer to get things decided, those with a preference for judging may already have a solution in mind when they come to discuss the conflict. Often they will assess others' ideas in relation to their preferred solution. Entering the deliberations with a plan in mind no doubt makes it easier for them to work toward resolution fairly quickly.

As people who prefer to continue to gather information and consider options, those with a preference for perceiving are often able to see several viewpoints and propose alternative solutions. Rather than bringing a solution with them, they await to see what emerges from the discussions. Instead of moving more definitely toward a conclusion, they prefer to remain open until the various ideas and opinions have been considered. Who knows? A totally new concept may emerge from the various perspectives presented.

Here are some brief illustrations of how judging and perceiving can affect our responses to conflict.

- Two Js in conflict may need to be aware of agreeing on a solution too quickly (without, for

Putting Type to Work

example, consulting others who may be affected or considering many different alternatives). "Sleeping on it" could be a helpful strategy for them.

- Two Ps may need to be explicit about when agreement has been reached and consciously agree to stop processing after that point, otherwise the conflict will seem dragged out as though it is never-ending.
- A common frustration between Js and Ps occurs when the Js think a decision has been reached (i.e., a particular solution or a course of action has been agreed to) while the Ps regard it as "still baking" and subject to modification. Agreeing to a trial period, after which the resolution can be fine tuned and then solidified, may be helpful in this situation.

Work Style

Different types work differently. They work at different paces, seek varying amounts of external stimulation and interaction, and view work and play from contrasting perspectives.

Pace

People with a preference for sensing often have a work pace that differs from those with a preference for intuition. Sensing types typically work at a steady pace. Given a project that will take three days, for example, a sensing type—particularly an SJ— is likely to dig right in and complete a portion of it each day, perhaps finishing it early. In contrast, intuitive types—particularly NPs—are more likely to have periods of high energy and productivity followed by apparent lulls. A three-day project may be undertaken in a day, a half-day, or ....

J and P can also affect work pace. People with J as the last letter of their type formula like to finish things and tend to want to narrow the alternatives pretty quickly, whereas people with a preference for perceiving like to start things and to remain open to additional information and options as long as possible.

Js are often not excited about beginning new projects, but become more engaged as a plan unfolds and is implemented. Their first reaction may well be, "I don't see how I could fit that into my schedule right now". Though later they might announce, "I've re-arranged my schedule and will be able to be involved after all." Once started, they are likely to want to stick with a project and devote their energy to it until its conclusion even though other needs may become evident. More excited by finishing than starting, they are ready to celebrate when the project is done.

More naturally open to what comes along, Ps typically welcome the chance to get involved in something new. "That sounds like fun!" might be their first response. As a project evolves, they may also seem to become diverted as they devote energy to other new, interesting things which come along. More excited by starting than finishing, they may need to push themselves to get a project finished, and may actually experience a little let down when it is all wrapped up. While the Js feel like celebrating, the Ps wonder what's next.

Of course, it isn't as simple as only describing the effects of J and P on one's approach to work. As the elements of type combine, the type equation becomes more complex. For example, EJs are decisive and action-oriented. While the IJs may ponder and be circumspect, the EJs usually want to take some steps to move the project toward completion, even though their plates are full and they feel as though they can't possibly do one more thing. So EJs may feel torn between wanting to get going and not wanting to start something new which they will feel compelled to carry through to closure.

On the other hand, IPs are reflective and adaptable. Before becoming involved they may want to think about it longer than the EPs. Even though it might be important or interesting, it will require putting energy into the outer world, something many introverts are cautious about. So for IPs the tug is likely to be between the appeal of something new and interesting and the caution of jumping in without having thoroughly thought it through.

Putting Type to Work

Interaction and Interruptions

Introverts describe themselves as liking fairly long periods of time for concentration. Someone or something that interferes with the concentration is experienced as an interruption. Liking to concentrate entails staying in one place. Extraverts look for something of interest in the outer world, so what is an interruption to an introvert may be welcome stimulation or a break to extraverts. If there isn't much of interest in their immediate surroundings, extraverts may go in search of it and hence are often seen out and about, in interaction with others.

Work and Play

How serious or playful the climate should be is a consideration that may arise. Judging types often take their work pretty seriously, and they may make a clear demarcation between work and play. For them, completing one's work precedes play. "Why do you think they call it work?", with its implicit message that work is supposed to be serious and hard, might well have been uttered by someone with a preference for judging, possibly a TJ.

Perceiving types, on the other hand, are much more likely to intermix work and play. If their work isn't fun, they'll find a way to introduce playfulness. It's not that they don't get their work done, it's just that they want to have some lightheartedness along the way. Our type preferences have undoubtedly influenced our responses to recent changes such as casual dress days or workshops about injecting humor into the workplace.

Team Processes

Type can come into play in nearly every element of a team—what happens during the stages of team formation and functioning, who tends to assume particular roles, the various images that members hold of the "ideal team", the differing values placed on meetings, how the team makes decisions and deals with conflict, and the communication patterns that develop.

The process that a collection of individuals goes through to become a team is often delineated in four stages originally described by Bruce Tuckman—forming, storming, norming, and performing. While working through the earlier stages, groups spend more time on the process or relationship aspects of a team. The later stages are more focused on the work and tasks.

Team members' type preferences interplay with these developmental stages.

Forming: Coming together and beginning to form into a group or team is a process that involves time spent learning about one another and beginning to form relationships. Hence, it is much more interesting and important to those types which are people and process-oriented and which tend to do their best work when they feel a sense of relationship with their co-workers, particularly ESFPs and ENFPs. On the other hand, those who are more task-oriented and who place less emphasis on attending to group process and establishing relationships, e.g., ISTJ and INTJ, may be frustrated during this stage and want to get "down to business".

Storming: Storming entails coming to grips with the conflicts that inevitably arise within a group. How type preferences can impact our reactions to conflict is discussed under the heading Responding to Conflict on page 35. Some teams never progress much beyond this stage—and spend a lot of time rehashing the same issues—because they are unable to find ways of dealing productively with strife.

Norming: Figuring out what we expect of each other as group members and how we want to work together as a team is norming, the deliberate establishment of norms. Being more task-oriented, Js usually want to establish and work toward goals, objectives, deadlines, milestones, and schedules. To Ps, matters such as how the team will decide, who will be involved, and what information will be brought to bear on its deliberations are of greater interest and concern. Similarly Ss and Ns, notably SJ and NP, may differ in their approaches to planning, including how specific to be and what time frame to encompass. Those with preferences for sensing and for judging typically prefer more specific plans that cover shorter time periods, whereas those with intuitive and perceiving preferences favor less definite

Putting Type to Work

and more long-term strategies. (Team success no doubt involves developing both short- and long-term plans and strategies and also entails "convincing" both Ss and Ns of the need for both.)

Performing: Collaboration, synergy, enjoyment, and satisfaction in being part of a group that is clearly making progress characterize performing, those periods when the team is functioning quite well. From the perspective of type, performing occurs when each of the types can contribute their "gifts" and have them valued as a necessary and important contribution to the whole.

Meetings: Meetings are a common way for teams to get some of their work done. Team members with different type preferences usually view the value and functions of meetings differently. Talking something through with others often helps extraverts clarify their thinking, so they may find meetings helpful. Introverts typically come to understanding alone and may view meetings not as places where work gets done, but where more work is created that has to be done outside the meeting.

Meetings are also get-togethers where team members interact, socialize, and continue to get to know one another. Those with preferences for extraversion and for feeling typically appreciate this function of team gatherings more than other types. In contrast, ITJs may most value the task-oriented portions of meetings.

Decision Making

The zig-zag process, developed by Gordon Lawrence, is helpful in applying type to both individual and group problem-solving and decision-making processes. The steps in the process can be thought of as bases that need to be covered to make a sound decision.

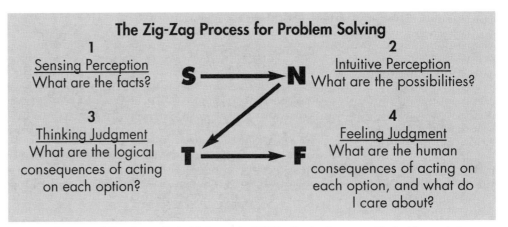

From *People Types and Tiger Stripes* (3rd ed.) Copyright 1993 by Gordon Lawrence. Used with permission.

As individuals, we are naturally interested in and drawn to two of the bases and much less interested in the others. (In *People Types and Tiger Stripes*, Lawrence calls this our "natural bias".) The two bases that call to us are represented by the middle two letters in our type formula; for some those are S and T, for others they are S and F, N and F, or N and T. We are prone to start the process and spend the bulk of our problem-solving time with our favorite steps. Similarly, we are less likely to spend much time on, and may even omit, the other two steps.

Each base takes us to an essential aspect of decision making.

The **S base** involves gathering specific data and attending to current reality (and considering factors such as how long we have had this problem, who is affected, what we have already tried, if we have budget available to help solve it).

The **N base** involves generating alternative courses of action and attending to future possibilities (and considering factors such as what we could do if we had no constraints, how would it be if things were exactly the way we'd like them to be, how this problem is like and unlike other problems we have faced).

The **T base** asks us to take into account the logical consequences of each alternative (and to

Putting Type to Work

consider factors such as the reasons for and against each possibility, what makes sense, what the data indicate, what the bottom line requires).

The **F base** asks us to take into account the affects of each alternative on the people involved (and to consider factors such as whether people will support or resist each alternative, what feels right, what the human "costs" are, and whether this course of action is congruent with our values).

When individuals or groups fail to adequately cover a base, a less than satisfactory decision often results. Here are a few examples from both personal and organizational life.

Several years ago, a couple I know needed to buy a new refrigerator. Together they naturally covered the N, T, and F bases. After reading *Consumer Reports* to discover their "best buy" recommendations, they headed off to Sears, home of one of the top three choices. After a brief chat with the sales person, they made their purchase and had it delivered. After using the new refrigerator for a while, they noticed that it seemed a bit too small and wished it had more room in it.

How had this happened? How had they managed to buy a refrigerator that was too small? The zig-zag provides an explanation. Though as a couple they encompassed the N, T, and F facets of making a decision, neither naturally attended to sensing. The size of the refrigerator—the number of cubic feet recommended for a family of four or five—was a detail that had eluded them.

The refrigerator incident was relatively inconsequential. Paying inadequate attention to or skipping steps in the zig-zag process can have more serious consequences, however. An ENFP entrepreneur got involved in a business venture to develop recreational land. She was excited about the prospect of spending time in the country and looked forward to having her friends buy plots there too. Naturally tending to cover the N and F bases of the zig-zag, she herself paid only scant attention to the S or T bases, nor did she engage professionals, such as attorneys or accountants, who might have helped her do that. Not having attended very closely to some of the "realities of business" (e.g., legal documents, cash flow requirements), she ended up losing a considerable amount of money.

To illustrate how the zig-zag can apply to "bottom line" decisions, consider two prominent, multi-million dollar business decisions made by large organizations. One was the decision to introduce New Coke™ and its eventual removal from the market because the U.S. public did the unthinkable by rejecting a "new and improved" version of a product. The other was Johnson & Johnson's much lauded handling of the Tylenol® tampering incident. Though the problem was apparently confined to a particular geographical area of the U.S., Johnson & Johnson officials invited consumers from across the country to return their product for a refund or replacement.

Although I have no "hard" data to support this analysis, it seems as though how these decisions would affect people—the F base in the zig-zag process—was weighted quite differently in these cases. From the outset, Johnson & Johnson seemed to have considered the "impact on people" whereas Coke gave it too little weight (or perhaps bypassed it altogether) with rather costly consequences.

ISTJ ■■	ISFJ	INFJ	INTJ
ISTP ■	ISFP	INFP	INTP
ESTP	ESFP	ENFP	ENTP ■
ESTJ ■■	ESFJ	ENFJ ■	ENTJ

A team can use the zig-zag to reveal areas that need more conscious attention paid to them. One way to do this is to select two decisions, one which was successful and another that didn't turn out the way they wanted it to, and then to describe how each step of the process was actually carried out for each decision.

Consider a seven member team with the following make up: 2 ISTJs, 2 ESTJs, 1 ISTP, 1 ENTP, and

Putting Type to Work

1 ENFJ. Since five people on the team prefer sensing and six have preferences for thinking, this team would probably craft solutions that are logical, sensible, data-based, and grounded in reality. Whether or not the N and F bases get sufficient consideration—i.e., whether they examine sufficient alternatives before deciding and weigh how their decisions will affect people—could depend on how the ENTP and ENFJ are regarded. Are they able to make themselves heard because of their preferences for extraversion? When they contribute, are they respected and listened to because they have perspectives and information that is important, or are they disregarded because their viewpoints often run counter to what the others think?

The roles and power within the group are also factors to take into account. If one of the ESTJs were the leader of this team, a very different dynamic could occur than if the ENFJ were. With an ESTJ as leader, the press to make ST decisions might be felt even more strongly. With an ENFJ as leader, the F perspective would probably take on more significance, though there might also be tension between the NF and the STs.

Professional or organizational roles can be an additional influence. If this were a small accounting firm with the STs as accountants and the others in support roles, the ST way would probably be clearly evident. On the other hand, if it were a marketing research department with team members occupying peer positions, more balance—or tension—might emerge.

Change

In most organizations, change has been the dominant theme for the last two decades and will continue to be for the foreseeable future. For both individuals and organizations, being able to navigate change successfully is an important skill for thriving. The chart "Type and Change" summarizes how the dimensions of type can influence the approaches to change taken by individuals, groups, teams, and entire organizations.

A group's or organization's inclinations during change can also be examined using Earle Page's *Organizational Tendencies* which indicates the basic posture toward change often taken by people in the four quadrants of the type table.

Organizational Tendencies

IS "Let's keep it"	IN "Let's look at it another way"
ES "Let's get it done"	EN "Let's change it"

From *Organizational Tendencies* by Earle Page.

Two things can happen when a team has few representatives of one of the types or type-related groupings. One possibility is that team members are aware of and appreciate everyone's gifts and recognize the gifts of the less represented types as necessary for the group's success. Alternatively, the differences may be neither appreciated nor valued, but rather become a source of confusion and contention. The gifts of the minority are not only unappreciated but they are also seen as an impediment to progress.

If a team lacks representatives of one of these type-related groups, they may want to be deliberate about providing the perspectives and information that are missing. With some conscious effort, team members themselves may fill in the gap, or the viewpoints of others outside the group may be sought.

Consider, for example, a team that has five people in the IN group, three in the EN group, one in the IS group, and none in the ES group. What might we hypothesize about this team? They would probably have a lot of ideas for change and might well be seen as one of the innovative groups in their organization. However, implementation of the ideas and follow-through to make things happen could

Type and Change

Extraverts

- Take prompts and impetus from external environment
- See others as an important resource
- Communicate with others throughout the process
- Move ahead more quickly—action-oriented

Introverts

- Take prompts and impetus from inner thoughts and standards
- See themselves as the basic resource
- Think things through—communicate little until decision has been made
- Move ahead more slowly—oriented to reflect

Sensing types

- Look to the present and past for guidance; tradition and current practices are important factors
- Propose change which builds on what already works, and want data or experience to support the new direction
- Change when the realities of the situation dictate

Intuitive types

- Look to the future for guidance; what could be is an important factor
- Propose large scale, sweeping, sometimes dramatic changes, and are comfortable proceeding based on a model, general idea, or hunch
- Change to try new things, be different, or get something going

Thinking types

- "What" is more important than "how" (the process)
- May de-emphasize or overlook the "people" part; expect change to be disruptive, ruffle some feathers
- Try to be objective, even about personal change, and base actions on principles

Feeling types

- "How" (the process) is equal to or more important than "what"
- The "people" part is a first and fundamental consideration; prefer to have harmony during change
- Personal, subjective values form the basis for change

Judging types

- Want to get things decided, wrapped-up— may push for a conclusion
- View change as something to be managed or controlled; may be thrown off by unanticipated events
- Prefer to have a plan or structure to provide direction and an orderly process; approach change with an idea of what is "right" or "best"

Perceiving types

- Want to keep options open—may want to delay reaching closure
- View change as an organic process that will evolve over time; expect surprises and are OK with letting the process unfold
- May regard specific planning as unnecessary and limiting; are open to new approaches that become evident as the process evolves

Putting Type to Work

well be a challenge for this group because it has such a clear predominance of members preferring intuition. They might also be viewed as ignoring what has already been shown to work, i.e., as "throwing the baby out with the bath water."

A different dynamic would probably occur if the team expanded and added two people in the ES group and one more in the IS quadrant. To begin with, it is likely that the group will cycle back through the stages of team development, and experience storming when the new members put forth their approaches. The ESs and INs may begin to experience tension, as one group presses to take action and the other seeks to assure that all the relevant perspectives and options are taken into account. Similarly, with more of a voice in the expanded team, the ISs may favor change which deliberately builds on what already works whereas the ENs would likely push for more large scale, possibly dramatic innovations.

Type helps us have our radar up to look for particular, predicted dynamics, but we must always test our predictions against what actually occurs because it is possible that none of these expected dynamics would be evident. Once we know the actual issues faced by a team, type can assist in planning, introducing, and sustaining change.

Communication

Communicating effectively is challenging under the best of circumstances —and much of the communication we have each day is not conducted under those kind of conditions. Type can help us get some of the "noise" out of our communications, removing unnecessary barriers to satisfying and productive interactions.

We can think of different types as using different languages and of a corresponding need to translate in order to communicate. For example, when speaking about a team's or organization's directions for the future, those with a preference for intuition may speak of "creating a vision" while people with a sensing preference may talk about "formulating goals and objectives." Similarly, during assessments of individuals or teams, thinking types may point out "weaknesses" while feeling types see "areas for improvement" or "opportunities for growth."

Knowing type can assist in planning and improving communication by helping us become aware of our own natural style and "language" and also alerting us of what to expect from others. Here are some communication behaviors and characteristics that are often associated with each element of type.

- People who prefer extraversion are often dynamic, animated communicators; they process externally so you know what they are thinking; they prefer to communicate directly with others.

- People who prefer introversion are reflective, low key, less demonstrative communicators; since they process internally and verbalize only the results, they provide less information and you are less likely to know how they reached their conclusions and may experience lapses in communication while they process; they are comfortable communicating indirectly via memo, electronic mail, etc.

- People who prefer sensing talk about and are interested in specific information derived from experience and offer evidence from past and present reality; they are drawn to usefulness (current potential), communicate unambiguously, and provide exact accounts and actual examples.

- People who prefer intuition talk about and are interested in theoretical and conceptual information; they are excited by future potential, seem to communicate circuitously (jumping around and including unrelated points), and provide general accounts, (drawing associations, attending to figurative meaning, and providing few specifics).

- People who prefer thinking focus on the purpose and want to get down to business; they give the pros and cons, note deficiencies and make suggestions for improvement when others put forth ideas.

- People who prefer feeling focus first on the relationship and take time to attend to it; they appreciate the contribution of all perspectives, affirm and build on areas of commonality, and seek agreement when others put forth ideas.

- People who prefer judging focus on reaching closure, on finishing things; they readily come to the point and present opinions that make it seem as though things are already settled for them.

- People who prefer perceiving focus on gathering information and looking at options; they explore a variety of viewpoints and alternatives before coming to the point; and they present perspectives that make it seem as though things are flexible and open-ended.

Putting Type to Work

Have you ever pondered the challenges of communicating with your typological opposite? My own type is INTJ and my opposite type is ESFP (because "E" is the opposite of "I", "S" the opposite of "N". "F" the opposite of "T", and "P" the opposite of "J"). Let's say that my boss is my opposite, and I have a proposal to make that I really want her to approve. How should I approach the presentation?

I would plan to present my proposal face to face and be ready to convey the enthusiasm I might usually keep inside. Depending on how long it has been since she and I have talked, I would expect to spend some time catching up with one another before getting down to our business.

I would need to pay particular attention to the specifics that I might usually not give primary consideration. For example, if there are costs involved, I would want to have defensible estimates and accurate (not approximate or ballpark) figures. I would also want to include more detail about how the project would actually be carried out than I myself would usually have specified by this point.

I would want to be sure to address how the project would affect people (e.g., perhaps it would eliminate a troublesome bottleneck or it might require a few people to work until 6:00 p.m. each day). Speaking with a few employees ahead of time to get their reactions to my proposal would allow me to incorporate their actual feedback into our discussion.

My typical style would be to present the proposal in a structured manner, probably going through each section in order. I will need to be patient if my boss doesn't necessarily stick to my structure; she might loop back to previous sections or take what seem to me to be tangents. Even though I am enthusiastic—and by now I hope my boss is as well!—I wouldn't necessarily expect a decision to result from our meeting. Wanting to give it some consideration, perhaps running it by some other people, would be a more likely response. If a decision seemed to be reached, I would regard it as still subject to modification at this point.

You should recognize that communicating like this would be hard for me (as communicating with your opposite would be for you) because it requires conscious attention to alter my natural communication style and to pay heed to those elements of type to which I customarily give little energy.

Of course, it would be impractical to communicate this deliberately in each of the interactions we have each day because it would take too much time and energy. Fortunately, much of our communication works, i.e., it is effective and satisfying. It is when communication isn't working that making deliberate use of type can be helpful. Often when our natural style isn't effective we just do more of what we are already doing—we talk more loudly, typologically speaking. For example, an ST naturally provides objective data, and if objective data doesn't convince the recipient, s/he may go and get more of the same kind of data unless s/he steps back to ask, "What does this person need to hear that I am not providing them?" The STs are not the only ones with this kind of liability; the SFs, NFs, and NTs each also have potential blindspots about their own preferred kind of information.

Occasionally when I suggest adapting communication this way, someone is concerned that it seems manipulative. I usually make two responses. The first is this. If you are going to give flowers to someone, and their favorites are tulips but you like roses, which kind will you send? Nearly everyone says tulips. That's what this is about—sending the person what they really want. If I want my boss to approve my proposal, I'd best address her concerns and include the kind of information it takes to convince her. (Of course, just sending her preferred kind of information does not in itself guarantee approval!) Secondly, I advise that if it seems manipulative, don't do it.

Many people face the challenge of communicating with others whose type preferences they do not know or with groups of anonymous people. In these situations, Gordon Lawrence's zig-zag process, discussed more fully under Decision Making, can be helpful. The four elements of that model comprise a "complete message" from the perspective of type. Such a message

- presents the specific facts of current experience and past reality—what is and has been—for those who prefer sensing,
- presents the big picture, future possibilities and interpretive meanings—the "what ifs"—for those who prefer intuition,

Putting Type to Work

- considers the objective factors and logic—what "makes sense" and doesn't make sense—for those who prefer thinking, and
- considers the subjective factors and human ramifications—what "feels right" and doesn't feel right—for those who prefer feeling.

Two good examples of typologically "incomplete" messages appeared in ads in the August 7, 1995 *Fortune* magazine. The first is a two page ad. On the left hand page is a women standing on the top of what appears to be a desert canyon. She is dressed in hiking clothes, holding a walking stick, and gazing intently off into the horizon. Approximately the top 80% of the right hand page is taken up by 10 words in large type—"visionaries, wizards, dreamers, pioneers, philosophers, ideas, ideals, aspirations, information, innovation"—followed by the name of the company in the same size type. The five sentences of text at the bottom of the page include "we do share a common goal: a better world for future generations." Other than a reference to "technology", the ad does not indicate what business the company is in.

Contrast this with another ad just a few pages away. The top half of this page is taken up with a quote from Stephen Sondheim: "Everything depends on execution, having just a vision is no solution." The copy goes on to talk about turning dreams into reality. It is clear what business the company is in, and a name and phone number are provided.

No doubt these ads say much about the people who created them and who purchased them, and they appeal to very different types of readers. The first one projects intuition. It focuses on the future, provides words apparently intended to evoke associations, and contains few specifics. The second reflects sensing. It talks about reality and about the limitations of imagination (i.e., vision), promises solutions, and even gives the name and phone number of a specific person to contact.

Next time you get a flier soliciting your business, or listen to a public figure urging a particular course of action, or react to an advertisement, try using the zig-zag to see how or if the communicator encompasses each element. Few communicators hit them all—and the communications that appeal to us usually have covered our favorites (i.e., the middle two letters of our type formula) whereas those communications that do not catch our attention have not.

Whether you are communicating face to face or to an unknown audience, you will probably be more successful trying to explain, influence, or convince if you deliberately cover all the "bases" of the zig-zag.

■ One need only look at the trouble spots in the world or the points of friction in our own worlds of work, neighborhood, and family to realize that acquiring effective ways to deal with differences is a pressing need. The Myers-Briggs Type Indicator can be very helpful in this process.

Isabel Briggs Myers invited us to regard the differences among us as "gifts" that each of us brings to the various settings we are in. Long before the emphasis we now give to diversity rooted in gender, race, ethnicity, and sexual orientation, she championed another kind of diversity, psychological diversity.

Being human, we don't always receive others' gifts as gifts. Sometimes they might be perceived as a challenge (How are we going to deal with the challenge of Jack's being such a stickler for details?) or a downright annoyance (It is so annoying when Amy keeps coming up with new ideas after we've already decided.)

Again, Isabel Briggs Myers had counsel for us when she observed "Any relationship will suffer if oppositeness on a preference is treated as an inferiority."

On our good days, may we regard people's talents and contributions as gifts. On our not-so-good days, may we see them as challenges. And may we never treat them as inferiorities.

Helpful Resources

The number of type-related resources that have become available over the past decade has grown to the point where it would be difficult to list them all. Here are just a few that will be helpful in taking a further look at type at work.

Nancy J. Barger and Linda K. Kirby. *The Challenge of Change in Organizations: Helping Employees Thrive in the New Frontier.* Palo Alto, CA: Davies-Black, 1995.

William Bridges. *The Character of Organizations: Using Jungian Type in Organizational Development.* Palo Alto, CA: Consulting Psychologists Press, 1992.

Sandra Hirsh (with Jane Kise). *Work It Out: Clues for Solving People Problems at Work.* Palo Alto, CA: Davies-Black, 1996.

Sandra Hirsh. *MBTI Team Building Program.* Palo Alto, CA: Consulting Psychologists Press, 1992.

Sandra Hirsh and Jean Kummerow. *LIFETypes.* NY: Warner, 1989.

Otto Kroeger and Janet Thuesen. *Type Talk At Work.* NY: Dell, 1992.

Jean M. Kummerow, Nancy J. Barger, and Linda K. Kirby. *WORKTypes.* NY: Warner, 1997.

Gordon Lawrence. *People Types and Tiger Stripes*, Third Edition. Gainesville, FL: Center for Applications of Psychological Type, 1993.

Gerald Macdaid, Mary McCaulley, and Richard Kainz. *Atlas of Type Tables.* Gainesville, FL: Center for Applications of Psychological Type, 1986.

Charles Martin. *Looking At Type and Careers.* Gainesville, FL: Center for Applications of Psychological Type, 1995.

Charles Martin. *Looking At Type: The Fundamentals.* Gainesville, FL: Center for Applications of Psychological Type, 1997.

Isabel Briggs Myers with Peter B. Myers. *Gifts Differing.* Palo Alto, CA: Consulting Psychologists Press, 1980.

CAPT also publishes several workshop and training handouts related to the topics discussed here.

Communication:

Susan Brock, *The Four-Part Framework*

Jean Kummerow, *Talking in Type*

Decision Making :

Gordon Lawrence, *The Zig-Zag Process for Problem Solving*

Change:

Earle Page, *Organizational Tendencies*

Work Style:

Isabel Briggs Myers, *Effects of Each Preference in Work Settings*

Gordon Lawrence, *I Do My Best Work When…*

Teams:

Mary McCauley, *Teamwork Analysis Exercise*

Mary McCauley, *Predictions About Teams*

Background Notes

About the Publisher

The Center for Applications of Psychological Type, Inc. (CAPT) was established in the summer of 1975 with two major goals: to help make what is already known about psychological types useful in practical ways and to create new knowledge. Its founders, Isabel Briggs Myers and Mary H. McCaulley, adopted "the constructive use of differences" as the motto for this non-profit organization.

CAPT educates the public and professionals to view differences constructively by maintaining a number of services for use in education, counseling, organizational development, religious life, and research.

- CAPT houses the Isabel Briggs Myers Memorial Library, the largest collection of MBTI® publications, dissertations, and theses in the world. The bibliography for the MBTI instrument is also maintained by CAPT Research Services.

- CAPT publishes and distributes papers and books related to research and practical applications of the Indicator. On-going research is conducted and made available through new products and services.

- CAPT computer scoring for the MBTI produces high-quality, professional reports. This service attracts a large number of MBTI users; it also facilitates the collection of MBTI responses, contributing significantly to original research on the study of personality.

- The training department of CAPT offers basic and advanced training worldwide for managers, educators, counselors, psychotherapists, career counselors, psychologists, organizational development consultants, and religious leaders.

For a catalog about all these services and products, contact CAPT.

Center for Applications of Psychological Type, Inc.
2815 N.W. 13th Street, Suite 401
Gainesville, Florida 32609
(800) 777-2278
E-mail: capt@capt.org
Website: www.capt.org

About the Author

Larry Demarest, Ph.D., (INTJ) is a trainer and organizational development consultant who has worked with the MBTI® personality assessment tool since the late 1970's. His primary use of the Indicator are in training, management, and organizational development, and team building. In addition to time management, he has done research on type and gender and also type and personal change. Larry is the author of *Out of Time: How the Sixteen Types Manage Their Time and Work*, he is on the CAPT training faculty and he is active in the Association of Psychological Type.

Notes

Notes

Notes

Notes